The Dear One Letters

A Path to Growing as a Human and Evolving as a Soul

Dr. Connie Numbers

The
Dear One
Letters

*A Path to Growing as
a Human and Evolving as a Soul*

DR. CONNIE NUMBERS

Volume One

Two Harbors Press

Two Harbors Press
212 3ʳᵈ Avenue North, Suite 290
Minneapolis, MN 55401
612.455.2293
www.TwoHarborsPress.com

ISBN-13: 978-1-937928-39-1
LCCN: 2012932267

Distributed by Itasca Books

Designed by Jeff Fahey
Typeset by Naate Meyers

Printed in the United States of America

You are a
Magnificent Light
in His world —

Dedication

This book is dedicated to the memory of June Burke, who spent much of her life "falling asleep" so the rest of us could awaken.

and

To the memory of my grandmother, Merta Bradshaw, whose patience, soft songs and sugar cookies rescued me as a child, and whose love continues to sustain me to this day.

Acknowledgements

Thank you, Dory Mayo, for your invaluable contribution to the creation of this manuscript and for your wonderful perfectionistic tendencies. You have helped to make this book everything I had hoped it would be. I am also grateful for your encouragement and support. May you continue to rejoice in your love for the tango and your life. It would be an honor if you would consider working with me again on the next book.

A special thanks to my family and friends for their love, support, and loyalty. Some of you have been with me every step of the way for years, and I feel grateful and blessed to have you in my life.

Because they contributed so much to my personal growth, I want to acknowledge my 3 analysts and my Seraphim angel. Thank you Rev. Ralph E. Fogg, Muriel Landesman, Dr. Kenneth Weissblum, and Julian. I thank all of you for teaching me how to rescue myself.

My heartfelt thanks to my patients, past and present, who continue to give me the opportunity to do what I love best and who give me the honor of sharing their life.

Finally, I want to acknowledge and thank the love of my life, Jeff Fahey, for being the wind beneath my wings, my Tarzan and Roy Rogers wrapped into one, and the soul who has come into this life with me to show me how to love more fully. Thank you, my love, for your patience. I know that some of our time together has been sacrificed because of the time needed to write this book. I am eternally grateful that you love me enough to help me follow my dream. You will always be my hero.

And thank you, God, for having the brilliant impulse to know Yourself by creating us all.

Table of Contents

Introduction

This is a book for *contemplation*. I do not ask that you believe everything you read, for these are *my* truths and life experiences. However, opening your mind to considering these truths could lead to viewing your life from an entirely different perspective and changing it for the better. Whether or not you use it to seek your spiritual self, this book has the potential to contribute to your happiness. Not only is it a psychological and spiritual guide, it is also a practical manual for everyday use.

Consider that each letter was written for you, because it was. This is a book meant to be lived, not just read. Test its wisdom by applying its principles, and see if they do make a difference in your life. It will serve you well if you read it from cover to cover at your own pace, reading and re-reading the letters slowly so as to get the full benefit of what each has to offer. It can also be used as a beacon that can guide you through any particular challenge you may have in life. Close your eyes, pose a question, wait, and then ask your soul to let your fingers open the book to a random page. What you need to know will appear on whichever page you turn to. All you have to do is trust and be open to what you see.

This is a book of *education*. Sections I and VII are based on the Julian teachings of the soul's journey throughout the continuum of time. Having experienced thirty years of sessions with Julian, I believe that these concepts frame an incredible masterpiece of understanding how the big picture works and how to make universal sense of life, love, and God. The book also addresses the spiritual principles of the law of attraction, which can help you understand how you are the Creator of your own life. Sections II through VI are the results of lessons I have learned that led me to love of self and to the discovery of my soul. These letters address the resistances within all of us that keep us from loving ourselves and leading happier lives. They teach us how fear can be turned into love, helplessness can be transformed into empowerment, and judgment can be released into the arms of compassion.

This is a book of *inspiration*. There is nothing more inspiring than joy, hope, and love. Each letter is filled with all that and more. This book is meant to activate a desire to think of yourself in a new and exciting way. It is also intended to help you re-think your version of who God is, moving away from a fearsome and punishing power, to a compassionate energy whose love has no end. My wish is that you feel inspired to believe that God lives within you and is only a breath away. In each letter, I have attempted to help you learn to ask the right questions, which in turn will help you find your own answers. Ultimately, I hope this book motivates you to believe that you are powerful enough to make a difference in the world by making a difference within yourself.

I do not believe that only a handful of human beings are meant to live lives of greatness or become masters of spirituality, and the rest of us need not apply. Yet, most of us do not believe that we are gifted enough, significant enough, or spiritual enough to create miracles, heal ourselves, or live spectacular lives. My wish is that you come to realize that nothing could be further from the truth. To know your Divine nature is your right, and all of us have been endowed from birth to do this and more. I encourage you to embrace that right. We are here to live a human life alongside the consciousness of our Divinity. My intent is to inspire you to discover how bright a Light you really are.

This is a book of *invitation*. I invite you to hear the voice of the soul that eagerly awaits you, your own soul. It is important for you to know that I am not special. My ability to hear my soul is not a special gift. Everyone has the ability to channel his or her soul at any time. Therefore, I am no more gifted than you are, and you can learn to distinguish your human voice from your soul voice without it taking thirty years. But to become proficient in anything, you must practice, practice, practice. This book gives you plenty of food for thought for that purpose. In fact, if you were to take only *one* letter and work on it for the rest of your life, everything in your life would change for the better.

Lastly, this is a book *for the rest of your life*. I invite you to keep it by your bedside. It is a wonderful feeling to go to sleep knowing that you are loved, and there is no end to the amount of love this book contains. Most of all, I invite you to seek the path of accepting your humanness, so you may live to be the extraordinary Light that you are. I wish you well on your journey, and I send each and every one of you my love and my blessings.

A Personal Preface

Ever since I was a child, I knew that something "big" was going to happen to me. I was sure that it must mean that I was going to be a famous singer or movie star. That's how irrefutable the feeling was. As years passed and fame and fortune did not come my way, I became confused and disappointed. What could this feeling have meant, if not that? "Maybe I made it up," I thought to myself. But I had not. This same feeling of "big" continued to haunt my psyche over the years. Difficult to describe, it was a knowing that I could not explain, an undeniable feeling of certainty. I knew, without a doubt, that something was coming. I just didn't know what, when, or how.

During the past year, while writing one of my letters, this feeling of "big" once again flooded my heart. At that moment, I suddenly had an epiphany, an "aha" moment of realization from out of the blue. I gasped and said aloud, "I know what it is! Here I am at this time in my life, writing a book about the process of remembering myself as a soul. I have some understanding of how life works on both a psychological and spiritual level. I am able to connect with the Divine in me and know, if only in the smallest way, who God is and what God feels like. And I finally know in my heart and soul that God and I are not separate. We are One. This feeling of "big" is my life, my journey. It's who I am. How could anything possibly be bigger than that?"

With that realization, I was able to see that I knew my destiny from the very beginning. I just didn't know what to call it, other than "big." Needless to say, I have not become a famous singer or movie star. Rather, I have turned into the person I always wanted to be. I cannot think of anything richer or blessed than that.

Other things that didn't make sense to me as a child are now crystal clear. Not only did I know something "big" was going to happen to me, but I also had the inclination that I was going to be of service, and this service would somehow be connected to God. For example, when I was eight years old someone asked me what I wanted to be when I grew up. I automatically replied, "A nun." To her surprise and mine, she said, "But you're not even Catholic," to which I replied, "What's Catholic?" In my child's mind the only women I had ever seen who lived a life serving God, whether in movies or in real life, were nuns. I interpreted that inner feeling of "service" by saying I wanted to be a nun, even though I had no clue about what a nun is or what a nun does. To this day, I am still amazed that a mere child could feel that Divine stirring within. In hindsight, I see that I have been guided on my path every step of the way. However, this path has not always been an easy one.

My life got off to a rocky start. Divorce was a rarity in the early 1950's, even more so if children were involved. Needless to say, my parents were one of the rare ones. They divorced when I was five and my father, for the most part, disappeared from my life until I was in my twenties. I loved him the most, and without him, I felt abandoned and utterly lost. Being the only girl in school with no dad was very difficult for me. I felt unloved, different, and jealous of every girl who had a father. I was left with a mother whom I feared more than I loved. I understand now that her need to rule out of fear was her way of preventing my brother and me from getting into trouble – and it worked. My mother had to hold a job outside the home to support us and was continually stressed about not having enough money. I'm sure that this in some way caused her mean-spiritedness. Although her nature was not warm and fuzzy to begin with, the anxiety of raising two children on her own must have been debilitating. Consequently, I too was debilitated by the absence of a father to protect me from her unhappiness and anger. While she was not without good qualities, she was hard-pressed to show them most of the time.

Throughout this disheartening childhood three things saved my emotional life. The first was my grandmother. She used to sit me on her lap in the rocking chair and sing to me, "Beautiful, Beautiful Brown Eyes," and "When It's Spring-time in the Rockies." I knew she was singing the first one about me, which made me feel very special. I still sing those songs from time to time. When she baked the most wonderful apple pies, she would shape the leftover dough into a little tart with a dollop of homemade strawberry jam on top, just for me. It was such a small gesture, but it meant the world to me. To this day, I still equate food with love. My grandmother was a patient, kind, and compassionate woman, and there was no doubt that she loved me. She was my first salvation. I've come to learn that love always delivers salvation. Although she died when I was sixteen, her effect on me was monumental, and to this day I can still feel her love.

My second rescuer was my brother, Ray. He is only eleven months younger than I, and many thought of us as twins. We looked alike and still do. Because I was born in December and he was born the following November, I used to tell people that we were only one month apart. That raised a few eyebrows. "Raymie" was my confidante, my playmate, and my partner in crime. When he got punished, I cried. When I got punished, he cried. It was a saving grace that we had each other and didn't have to go through life alone. What a blessing that was, and still is.

Last but not least, my life was saved by music. Both my parents were incredibly musical – my dad was a wonderful singer and my mother was an accomplished pianist. Musically, they were a great pair, but that was about it. At the age of ten, my talent for music was discovered by my fourth and fifth grade teachers, Mrs. Greenley and Mrs. Fee. (So you see, I did get "discovered" after all.) I could sing and play the piano so well that I was asked to perform in all sorts of venues – from talent shows, to musicals. Suddenly, the little girl who wore the same skirt to school for weeks, because it was the only one she had, stepped up into the world. And my mother, God bless her, somehow stepped up to the plate. Even though we had only popcorn for dinner on many nights, she managed to find the money to buy me performance outfits. To this day, I will never stop loving her for the dollar-and-a-half she gave me every week for piano lessons. So I can honestly say that she, too, saved my life. I just wish she would have let me love her as much as I wanted to.

By the time I was fourteen, my life took a huge turn for the better. My mother re-married and I acquired a new family, at least for the next ten years. High school had its ups and downs, but at least I was growing up, which was something I couldn't wait for as a kid. After high school I entered Ithaca College as a music student, and for the first time in my life, I felt free. After graduation, I spent eight joyful years teaching music. I loved being independent, loved teaching, loved my students, and they loved me. Their love had a profound effect on my life for that period of time. It was also during the first three years of teaching that I married and divorced.

It wasn't until I entered therapy in my twenties that I realized how wounded I was by my childhood and how I habitually covered up those wounds with a smile and a false mask of security. At twenty-six, I had no idea who I was or what I wanted, much less what I deserved. My sense of self was dependent upon whoever loved me at the time. The more people approved of me, the more lovable I thought I was. I was clueless and shocked at the revelations that came to me through my therapist, who spoke what seemed to be an entirely new language. What did he mean by *I* was responsible for my own feelings? How could he possibly insinuate that I was angry at my parents when there was not an angry bone in my body? (I still chuckle at that one.) And what made him think that I had unresolved issues? What did *that* mean, anyhow? Actually, he was telling me that I didn't feel good enough about myself and deserved to have better relationships. He said that if I would open up and tell him the story of my life, everything would change. He was right. Working with a competent therapist who knew me far better than I knew myself made for an amazing four years. Therapy was by far the best thing I ever did, because it paved the way for my growth, and I finally had someone willing to raise me in a loving and healthy way. I would have stayed in treatment longer, but I had an opportunity to tour the country as a singer in a rock band. I left my music teaching position and my French horn seat in the Hudson Valley Philharmonic, both of which I loved dearly, and for the first time in my life I left my comfort zone to take a risk. This was a "big" thing for me. I remained on the road for seven years out of the twenty in which I earned a living as a professional musician. I married the other singer in the band, my soul mate, Jeffrey, and off I went into one of the greatest experiences of my life. Today, three decades later, we continue to remain in love and live our life as an adventure.

Throughout those years I continued to work seriously on myself. I wrote constantly in my journals, recorded and analyzed hundreds of dreams, led dream workshops and seminars, and eventually earned a Master's Degree in Social Work to become a therapist. The feeling of "service" I had had as a child continued to permeate my soul, and I wanted to help others as I had been helped. In my early forties, I had the desire to dive deeper within myself, so I decided to enter therapy once again, this time with a different therapist. I continued with this for many years and later added another supervisor/analyst to help me become a more polished and competent therapist. To this day, he is still in my life and continues to support me. By the time I was fifty, I had earned a Doctoral degree in Psychology.

Being a psychotherapist for more than twenty-five years has taught me many things, one of them being that all of us have major turning points in our lives. I have already mentioned some of mine. There was, however, one extremely significant milestone that changed my life forever. More than any other incident in my adult life, this experience had the most profound and lasting effect on who I am. When I was twenty-five, I was introduced to an angel. Literally. One day a friend told me about a woman she visited for counseling who was a minister of the Church of Ageless Wisdom and a deep-trance medium. I had no idea what that was, but at the very least, it sounded like an interesting and fun thing to do. So I made an appointment to meet the Reverend June K. Burke. I will never forget the roly-poly woman who opened the door that day and giggled when she saw me. She then welcomed me with one of the warmest hugs I have ever had, putting me immediately at ease.

As I entered her office she said it was important for me to know all about her, what she did, and what to expect during this first session. She explained that she had been psychic as a child. She always knew who would be calling before the telephone rang and what things were about to happen on any given day. She thought every child knew these things, but when she began to grow up she discovered that others did not have this gift, so she stopped using her ability and eventually even forgot that she had it.

When giving birth to her son twenty-six years later, she suffered a postpartum hemorrhage and died. As she hovered above her body, she saw the look of compassion on the doctors' and nurses' faces as they worked on her. She felt no pain whatsoever. When she began to follow "the light," a voice asked her if she wished to fulfill her destiny. She had the choice of leaving the Earth experience or going back into this lifetime to fulfill what she came to do. She chose the latter because she thought it meant that she needed to raise her son. Upon making this choice, she was instantly transported back into her body and life on Earth. Soon after, she asked her doctor if she had, indeed, died giving birth. Shocked, he replied, "Yes. But how did you know that?" When she told him about her death experience, he said, "This is not the first time I've heard this." As an aside, June has always said that the death experience was the most beautiful experience of her life.

During the year after this incident, June and her friends formed a meditation group. She was fascinated with what had happened to her and wanted to know more about the mysterious world she had briefly seen. She remembered her childhood gift and was no longer afraid of it. Then one day, during one of their meditations, as June remained in the meditative state she was heard to say, "This is Julian." Upon awakening, she saw that everyone was staring at her. When they explained what had happened, June had no memory of it, yet knew that this was what she came back to Earthly life to do. In time, she understood that Julian was an angelic being who had worked with her as a child so she could fulfill her mission of helping Mankind. As the meditations continued, June and Julian's energies merged into one cohesive unit ranging from minutes to a few hours. For more than thirty years, June dedicated herself to serving anyone who needed and wished for Julian's counsel.

As fascinating as her story of that first session was, so were the chronicles of her counterpart, Julian. June explained to me that day that Julian is an angelic being, a Seraph of the order of Seraphim. From the beginning of time, he has bridged the two worlds that we call Heaven and Earth and has never incarnated. His sole existence and assignment is to be an emissary for God's messages and a deliverer of truths. June explained that all angelic forces were created by God to assist Mankind's growth so that we may remember who we really are and evolve into that being. She made it quite clear that Julian did not possess her. Actually, she had the power to deny him at any time. Rather, it was her own free will that permitted their energies to merge. She explained that Julian would not tell me what to do, but did have the ability to see my soul and the path I set forth before I got here. By having access to what she called the Akashic records, he would know about the past lives I have lived and would be able to ascertain if any of them were affecting this lifetime. He was ready and willing to answer any question I had about anything. With this in mind, I wondered if I had brought enough questions with me.

Before we started our first session, June commented that she would be amnesic during this time and would have no memory afterward of what she might say. Therefore, if I wanted to tape the session I could. As I popped my tape into the machine, June said her meditation to God and "went to sleep." It was then that I heard the words, "This is Julian," and for the next thirty years I heard these precious words more than a hundred times, and I have never been the same since.

Of course, what does a twenty-five-year-old want to know upon meeting an angelic being for the first time? Did I want to know about how life really works? Was I craving the secrets of the Universe? Did I want to know how I got here and who I was as a soul? Did it occur to me to ask about who God really is? Of course not! I wanted to know first and foremost about my past lives, especially if I had known the man I was currently in love with. I had to know if he really loved me, and would we have a future together? After all, to a woman of twenty-five, these are the quintessential questions of life, or so I thought at the time. More than once, Julian reminded me that the most important lifetime of my existence was the one I was currently in. I think he was trying to tell me something.

This first session paved the way for my eventual belief that Heaven and Earth can really meet and not only can God speak to us in many ways, but there are also many pathways to seeking God. Whatever question I had, Julian answered it to my satisfaction and added a few insights of his own. Since neither June nor Julian had ever met me before, I was quite surprised when he stated, "You have come into this lifetime, Connie, to use your creative abilities, for every soul is born from the creative Source. Although you were born to musical parents, you have also studied music on the spiritual plane, which has made you especially gifted in this area. You also have another innate talent – the skill of writing. This comes from having used this gift in your previous lives. Know that this ability is here for you should you choose to accept it," to which I thought, "Is he kidding?"

Julian asked if I wanted to be introduced to the three Spirit Guides who have come with me into this lifetime to help me on my journey. This was a new concept for me, so, of course I said yes. I was fascinated with the idea, but it wasn't until many years later that I truly understood how important my Guides would be.

The most incredible experience I had that day, however, was yet to come. Julian asked if I wanted to speak with a loved one who had crossed over. Immediately, I thought of my grandmother. He said he would send for her, but it would be up to her own free will to decide whether or not to come. There he was, talking about this "free will" thing again. I continued my questions until he announced that my grandmother was in the room. Hesitant, I said hello. I wasn't sure what to expect or if I really believed she was there. But when Julian relayed her message to me, I began to take this session much more seriously. I realized that I really might be in the presence of an angelic Divine being after all.

No one else could possibly have known about the things my grandmother mentioned. The details of her life were so explicit that, no matter how skeptical I felt, I could not deny that this was she. She spoke of her love for flowers, especially the beautiful roses that used to grace the side of her house. She talked about the songs she used to sing softly to me in her rocking chair and how she loved those times with me. She validated my unhappy childhood, but encouraged me to forgive my mother, asserting that she, too, had had it rough. She said she loved being back in her prime, now that she was no longer in physical form. She spoke of her passing and explained that it was not as bad as everyone thought. Laughing, she said that she wished she had remembered then what she knows now.

I was most impressed when she spoke of the service she has dedicated herself to on the spiritual plane. She sits at the bedside of children who are ready to cross over, and as a loving presence, helps them prepare for their passing. If anyone could ever comfort children, it was my grandmother. Then, she said with a chuckle, "Do you think, my dear, that once we die, we're just floating around here doing nothing?"

Grandmother ended our conversation by telling me how proud she is of me and that she has missed nothing in my life because she can be with me at any time. She wanted me to know that every time the thought of her suddenly pops into my head, at that moment she is there with me sending her love. After she blew a kiss and said goodbye, I had no doubt that I had been in the presence of my grandmother and privy to a miracle. I knew I would return again one day for another session, but I never realized I would return continually throughout the next thirty years.

During the early years of my sessions with Julian, I asked many questions that now seem somewhat superficial. However, as time passed and I began to mature, I asked more meaningful ones and learned about myself on a different level. I saw my childhood in a spiritual light and recognized how the struggle I suffered as a child led me to where I am today. I learned about soul growth and why our souls need to come back into the physical world. Everything about life, love, and God began to make sense in a way I had never imagined was possible. Over the next two decades, I had many sessions with Julian and attended some of June's workshops and retreats. I joined with others who were also enjoying the teachings of Julian. During this time, June's growing reputation attracted a number of lucrative opportunities, but she declined these offers in the belief that her service to others was more important than promoting herself. Eventually, she wrote three books based on the Julian teachings: "Self Creation and Manifestation," "Creation, Its Laws, and You," and "You Are Unique."

Being in the presence of Julian was like being in the presence of God. Every session left me feeling uplifted, joyous, loved, and filled with hope. June died seven years ago at the age of seventy-nine, and with her went Julian, who somewhere continues his work for the benefit of Mankind.

When I look back at my life, I can see how being nurtured by three therapists and an angel was a preparation for my "big" life yet to come. During those thirty years, I wrote diligently in my journal. My most intense writing streaks came when I would take a week off to go to Block Island by myself and write for hours each day. One day fifteen years ago, as I was sitting on the beach writing, my thoughts were suddenly interrupted by the words, "Dear One." I hesitated, because I didn't know where these words were coming from or why I was hearing them. Then I heard, "It's okay. Write down what you are hearing." So I wrote the words "Dear One" and continued to listen and write for most of the day. I kept hearing that it was okay to be skeptical about this experience, yet also important to accept it. All I had to do was to keep on writing. To be quite honest, my first reaction was one of trepidation. I knew that this voice was none other than my own, but it somehow felt different. While it sounded familiar, as though I had heard it many times throughout my life, this time it was clearer and more concise than ever before – peaceful, yet incredibly joyous. As I wrote, I had such a feeling of expansion that I almost believed I could fly away without a care in the world. I know now that I was feeling overwhelmed with love.

As I continued to write throughout the week, I allowed myself to listen to my voice without judgment. After a day or so, it didn't matter whether it was my human voice or the voice of my soul because I loved what I was hearing. I awoke every day feeling jubilant. In fact, I had never felt happier in my entire life. By the end of the week, I knew I was experiencing something quite magnificent. At first, I had a hard time believing that this could be happening to me. So for the next fifteen years I wrote voraciously, listening to this loving voice and learning to trust it. I never realized that I would eventually share these words, nor did I understand that the material for the Dear One letters was being created then and there.

When I contemplate who I used to be and who I am now, I am still amazed at the evolutionary process of life. Years ago, I came up with an analogy that describes my journey. It is this: I used to have a closet filled with thoughts, feelings, doubts, fears, and anxieties. In it also resided unresolved childhood issues, and unspoken wishes and dreams. This was my closet of "stuff." I've come to realize that all of us have a closet of "stuff." When I first entered therapy, the door of this closet was flung open, and all of the issues in the front of the closet came spilling out. It took a while for me to muddle through what had been blocking the doorway all this time, but I did. As those thoughts, feelings, anxieties, and fears became exposed, I was able to deal with them and step into the closet to see what else was in there. Oh, there were still lots of things on the shelves that needed to be thrown away, but at least now I could investigate them. As I continued my introspection, over time the closet became much less cluttered. I could actually walk around in it and feel freer than I had in years. There was still some stuff to contend with at the back of the closet, but there was also a tiny glimmer of light emanating from that area. As I grew to know myself in greater depth, the light became larger and larger. It began to take up more space than the darkness, until one day my closet was *filled* with this magnificent light of love. It was then I realized that the light had not increased in size at all. Quite the contrary! It had been huge from the very beginning, from the time I was born. I just needed to clean out all the stuff that had been blocking it, so I could see it. This light was my Divinity, my God self, my soul, just waiting for me to say "hello."

As I enter my early sixties, I can clearly see the unfolding of my transformation, how each step has led to the next, and how each level has deepened along the way. I know that every person in my life was placed in my path at the exact moment needed. And I finally understand why this book has not been finished earlier. Like me, it needed to be born in its right and perfect time.

In my earlier years, it never crossed my mind that formulating a loving relationship with myself would be the basis for my relationship with God. As I have become more attuned to my own Light, I have discovered a newfound freedom. I feel a greater sense of joy and hope, and I laugh spontaneously. I am less controlling toward myself and others. I no longer feel like the wounded child who thought she should have been born to different parents. Instead, I feel the excitement, spontaneity, and awe of an evolved child who is secure in knowing that I will always take care of her. And I finally realize that it was not my parents' job, at least in this lifetime, to give me the kind of security I was looking for. It was up to me to find it and give it to myself.

This book is "big" for me. It is the story of my life. It is the child I never had. It contains everything I am, everything I was, and everything I aspire to be. It covers the gamut of everything I've learned from more than thirty years of therapy and thirty years of wisdom from my spiritual mentor. I have poured every tear, every joyous moment, and every ounce of love I have into these letters. I could not give more of myself to anything if I tried. I never knew I had the capacity to love this much, nor did I know that I could put that love into words.

In essence, this is a book about love. It is a love story between a soul and its human personality. It is a story without an ending, for there is no end to God's love. I have come to know, from the bottom of my heart, that there is nothing "bigger" in life than love. It outlasts everything. And although this book was written for me, it was written for you, as well. My greatest wish is that you, too, consider that you are much bigger than you ever thought possible and worthy of the vastness of God's love within you.

Section I:

Open These Letters When You Want to Remember Who You Are, Where You Came From, and How You Got Here

I Am the "Forever" Part of You

Dear One,

From the moment you entered this lifetime, you were born all grown up. Housed inside that little body was a magnificent Light, a piece of the Creator, the Soul of you, ready for its journey into a world of dimension and potential, ready to fulfill its next purpose. You may have come into this life as a small package, but the contents inside were enormous and magnificently Divine. Those contents are Me, the Soul of you, your true identity – the most vital, precious, living part of you.

Since the moment of My creation, when God first breathed life into Me, I have been a Divine Consciousness. I am your ever-present connection to God because I am the living and Divine Presence of God within you. I am, literally, your sacred space and your holy spirit.

Therefore, I am here with you in this lifetime, living in two dimensions. I am a soul with the remembrance of who I am, and I also live in the world of form as a human being. I am the essence of God walking around as you. You take Me into every thought, feeling and experience you have, for there can be no separation between us. We are One. Yet, we have two separate energies, the human and the Divine. We are like a good peach, Dear One. The pit in the middle is Me. The savory sweetness of the peach is the goodness of God, and the skin of the peach is the humanness of you that holds us all together.

It is impossible to describe our relationship in one letter, which is why I have written a series of letters, so you can know and feel who you really are in the various walks of life. In this book I will continue to remind you of a very precious truth: I am your primary relationship. Whether you acknowledge Me or not, I am the most important connection you will ever have. There is no one more essential to get to know than Me, for in doing so are you given the opportunity to know your true self. When all is said and done, Dear One, it is Me, the forever part of you, who will continue to exist when this lifetime is over. What I am saying to you is that you do not have to wait for the death experience in order to remember the reality of you. As these letters will reveal, you can know Me now.

In this lifetime, you are My human counterpart, the human personality through which I experience life. I am here to evolve, and by coming back into physical form I am given this opportunity through you. You are the outfit I put on for a particular life, but the reality of who you are is not the outfit. Just as you, My human form, are the product of every thought, feeling and experience that has led you to where you are in this lifetime, so am I the product of every lifetime I have ever lived. Although I am having the Caucasian experience in this life, there is no race I have not encountered. Throughout My existence I have possessed the energies of both male and female, and while most of My lifetimes have existed on the Earth plane, some have been out of this realm, for the Universe is a vast playground for Creation.

There is no lifetime that is perfect, Dear One, nor is it supposed to be. In My human experiences, I have had lives of wealth and privilege, as well as deprivation and scarcity. Some lifetimes have lasted decades, others only days. Many have not turned out as I had hoped, yet in others I have reached great heights. Know this, however: There is never a lifetime of total failure for any soul. No matter what the outcome, there is always something learned in every lifetime. From each I have taken something that has added to My evolution, for I am always in motion, ever expanding and constantly creating. This is who God is. This is what God does. The beauty of

4

eternal life is that it gives every soul the opportunity to experience creation and growth in a new and different way across the span of time. This is how we evolve.

This lifetime with you, Dear One, is the most important lifetime of My existence. The many past lives I have lived make no difference. The most important lifetime for any soul is the one they are currently living, for it is the next stage in the process of their evolution.

I know it is not always easy to think of yourself as an eternal vibrational being who has existed for eons, but that is exactly who you are. You are not just a product of this lifetime because you are not that small. You are an expansive presence on this Earth that has never stopped living. You are the Universe. You are vast. You are so much more than you can ever imagine.

And so, when you took your first breath, our journey together began. I brought with Me every lifetime I have ever lived, every experience worth remembering, every lesson I have ever learned, and every ounce of wisdom ever gained. Thus, you were born knowing everything. You have been empowered since the day you were born and will remain empowered until the day you leave. With that empowerment comes the ability to have whatever you need and to be whatever you need to be at any point in time in your life. As I said, from the moment you entered this lifetime, you were born all grown up.

To tell you through language how I came to exist in the form of you is difficult. Because no language can adequately describe the spiritual, which is formless, this would be like trying to describe air. Telling you about the evolution of who I am and the process of getting here will be, at best, a simplified version of what can be understood by the human mind. Yet, all we have to work with is language. Therefore, I will do My best to express how I came into being and how each soul in its own unique way experiences this magnificent process of being human and Divine.

As a child, Dear One, it delighted you to no end to receive even the smallest gift – a butterscotch candy, a paper doll, a kind word. For much of your life you have had an underlying wish for the ultimate gift, a legacy. The desire to be left something special has found its way into your heart many times. Out of My love for you, I grant you your wish. These letters are My legacy to you. They contain all the knowledge, hope, compassion, inspiration, love, and wisdom I have to give. What brings this book to life is your belief in it and your willingness to listen and put the pen to paper. This gives you the right to have this book, this legacy of love, and to leave your own legacy to those who share in reading it.

Always remember this, Dear One: As you go through life, open this book to any page at any time, whenever you need to remember and feel the presence of who you really are. Know that you are a Divine being who exists in this space and time for a Divine reason. You have been given the Divine Mind of the Creator to summon up your energy and power for that purpose. You have been given Me as your Home away from home. And so, with love, in these next letters I will show you who I am, where I came from, and how I got here. In other words, I will reveal the beauty, awe, and wonder of you.

God Was Out to Give Himself Away

Dear One,

The other day, I watched you hunched over your desk, head in your hand, vexing over this particular letter. You could feel Me nudging you to include this letter in the book, but you also felt great resistance. You sat with pen in hand waiting for the answer to the age-old question, "How do I describe God?" As you wrote that single thought on a piece of paper, you examined it as a problem you could never solve. I could see the expression of frustration and doubt that you should even attempt to include this letter, because you knew inherently that it would not be good enough to answer that profound question. And you were right. There is no adequate description or definition of God that can tell the complete truth of who or what God is. In fact, there is no explaining God. As soon as you try, you have lost the actuality and essence of God. There are no words in this language or any other that can describe the totality or magnanimity of the Source of all Creation. It is utterly impossible.

Mankind has been looking to define God since civilization began, and each culture throughout time has had its own images and explanations of who God is. So it is no wonder you felt overwhelmed. You thought you were being required to do the impossible.

When you returned to your desk the next morning, hoping to throw this letter away, you saw the imposing question staring up at you. As you read, "How do I describe God?" three words popped into your head, "from the heart." That was Me, Dear One, giving

7

you the best answer to a question that cannot be answered. I flooded your mind at that moment, because I knew I must make the attempt in this book not to define God to you. One cannot define something that has no boundaries. Rather, I want to help you understand the essence of God, for in so doing, you will understand the true reality of Me living inside of you.

I also knew that in this letter I would have to address the word, "God." Although that particular word is the most common usage for describing the indescribable, throughout these letters I will refer to God by many names. I will speak of "The Almighty," "The Creator," "The Source of All That Is," "Divine Presence," "Great Spirit," and more. I happen to know you favor the word, "Father," because it comforts you and makes you feel as if you have one, which is all right. I resort to these various titles for God to steer you away from the concept that God is a "He." God is not the image of Man. Therefore, Dear One, know that when I do use the word, "He," or even the word, "God," it is only because this usage is familiar to you and your world, and it can make the essence of My message flow more smoothly. In the end, it doesn't matter by what name I call "God," for it is not the word, "God," that needs to be changed; it is one's perception of God that needs to change.

From My point of view, God is "The One." Everything in the Universe makes up the Oneness, but God is, "The One." The Infinite Creator is the universal energy of love that ties the Universe together. And you were formed from this very substance and energy. It is your source of all supply. Everything you are and everything you have comes from God. You can call the Heavenly Father/Mother any name you want, but know that if you do not understand that the essence of God is *within* you, then you are missing the most important aspect of who God is. If you look up to the sky and talk to God because you think this is the only place He lives, then you are not understanding the most beautiful and truthful part of who God is and who you are. So, it is not of great significance what you call God. My message to you is that it is more important how you *feel* God.

And God *is* from the heart, Dear One. When you feel love for another, you are feeling the love of God within you. When you feel love from another, you are feeling the love of God for you. There is no Love other than God's love. There are no varieties of love that are separate from the Creator. All love begins and ends with The Source of All That Is. Saying that "God is the feeling of unconditional love" even pales in comparison with the truth of what actually is. I know it is hard to fathom this kind of love, but this kind of love does exist. It exists within you and it exists for you. It is you.

I would like you to do something for yourself right now. Sit back for a moment and think about the love that has come into your life. Think of the gifts given to you physically, emotionally, and spiritually. Ponder the moments in which you have ever loved anything or anyone. Take into account all the acts of kindness you have given or received. Recall every song you have ever sung with joy. Remember those who have told you they love you, as well as those whom you know love you, although they may never have said it in words. Remind yourself of every animal you have ever loved and who has loved you back. Imagine every tender moment you've ever had with another, with Nature, or with yourself. Think of anyone who has said the exact word you needed to hear at the exact moment you needed to hear it. Think of when you laughed so hard you couldn't catch your breath. Think of the times, when feeling alone, you cried out. Then suddenly you felt a blanket of warmth, a Presence that comforted you.

Feel these moments of love. When you can catch even the smallest glimmer of love that has come your way throughout your life, you are just scratching the surface of feeling who God is and knowing who you are. Dear One, your "Father" has been here all along, for you could never have felt those moments of love without the Source of All Creation living inside you.

When God first breathed life into all souls, He made the decision to give Himself away. He gave out all of the pieces of Himself to create everything in the Universe. It was the greatest act of Love ever brought into existence. From that moment, I was born a soul, a Spark from the Great Fire; with that, I became the consciousness of God. And so the very fact that you exist is evidence of God's Love. It is why I could not let you discard this letter, Dear One, because God giving Himself away is the greatest love of all time, the greatest love story ever told. Like God, in your own unique way, you are also here to give yourself away, to give out pieces of yourself – pieces of love, so that you may continue to know yourself as you really are, the Presence of Magnificent and Eternal Love.

You Are Always Moving Up

Dear One,

Everything that was ever created evolves. The whole of creation evolves as a spiral. Throughout the Ages, this evolutionary spiral often repeats itself. Each repetition progresses to a higher level, toward greater understanding and greater accomplishment, because the natural progression and evolution of every soul is to move upwards. If you liken the spiral to a screw, for example, you would see the grooves of the screw go up and up, around and around, until they reach the top. This is what evolution looks like.

The importance of talking to you about your spiritual evolution is to tell you that it is your major purpose for being here. Every soul in human form is here for one purpose only, to move up. Evolving is the most important purpose for any soul. It is the reason every person who walks this Earth exists. How each soul accomplishes this with its human counterpart is as unique and varied as each star in the sky. This is the beauty of evolution.

Let me explain simply, Dear One, what I mean by "evolve." When you were a young child in the first grade, you sat in the second row, watching Mrs. Widrig put huge letters on the chalkboard, "A-B-C," and so forth. You had no idea where she was going with this, but eventually you began to learn that certain sounds went with each letter. One day, it seemed as if a miracle had happened. You finally understood that "C" plus "A" plus "T" sounded like and, was in fact, the word, "cat." From that moment on, a whole new world opened up for you. In time, words turned into sentences, and the wish to know more than sentences turned into stories, which have given you great pleasure throughout the years.

The desire as a child to want more than just the "ABC's" sparked a spiral of learning that has never ceased. From childhood you evolved to adolescence, and then to the various phases of adulthood. You continued to learn, but at higher levels of understanding. This was the natural course of your human evolution.

As your soul, I evolve in the same manner, except that I evolve spiritually. I have come into this Earth plane to bring what I already know to a higher level and let it evolve as far as it will go. In doing so, it brings new levels for Me to achieve. I have taken all the "ABC's" I know from My experiences as a soul, and have brought them to a new point in time, this lifetime. This means that I gain new understandings of those lessons at a higher level. As souls, we are not satisfied merely with knowing the letters of the alphabet either. We want the sentences, the stories, the experiences, and the adventures of life in order to know ourselves as Creators who have the ability to create and be whatever we want. This is our spiritual evolution.

Dear One, it is important for you to know that in the classroom of life there is no perfect "grade." Perfection itself is forever in the process of evolving. A perfect score in second grade is not the same as a perfect score in ninth grade. Some souls are here on a second grade level doing second grade work, which is "perfect" for them. Others are in fifth grade, and still others are in eleventh. One is no better than the other. You would never think of criticizing a second grader who could not do ninth grade work, which is why no person should be judged. Each of us is in the grade level in which he or she has arrived through personal evolvement. Not only is this okay, it is also the way it's supposed to be. And by the way, do not think that evolvement is discriminatory. Do not think that someone who appears to be living what people call a "lower life" is a lower being at a lower evolutionary stage. Clearly, there are many living at the poverty level who are in the ninth grade, and some CEO's in the second .

So when we, as souls, fulfill the purpose we set out to accomplish in this classroom of life, we move on to higher levels with more opportunities and more stories. Every lifetime gives Me the opportunity to choose again and again whether or not I can awaken you to remember who you are while in physical form.

When My time is up in this lifetime, Dear One, I will take the "ABC's" from this life and create new stories, new adventures, and new understandings at a higher level. Round and round I will go, up the spiral of evolution, until I reach My destination. Not even I know when that will be and what will happen when I get there. It doesn't matter. What I do know is that it will happen in its right and perfect time for the perfect unfolding of Me. God would have it no other way. It's His brilliant plan for all of us.

God Is the Architect, Not the Puppeteer

Dear One,

One of the greatest misconceptions in your world revolves around the concept that God is a being who decides what is going to happen to you, and what is going to happen to your world. For thousands of years Mankind has made God responsible for its fate, calling it God's Will. It has been assumed that God must have His own reasons for doing what He does. Since there can be no complete understanding of the Creator while we are in human form, this kind of thinking can create confusion and misunderstanding. It is difficult to comprehend why God's Will causes one person to die of cancer and another to recover, or why one child has a shorter lifespan than another. It is mind-boggling to wonder how people in one part of the world suffer depravity while those in another part experience great abundance. For many, the only answer that makes sense is to believe that God must have wanted it this way; otherwise it would not exist. With that prevailing mindset comes the belief that God must have His own agenda, and none of us are here to understand or question it.

Because much of Mankind has lost touch with its Divine Nature, it does not remember what it already knows, which is that God is the Architect of our existence, not a puppeteer who controls it. God is the Master Originator, The One responsible for creating The Grand Design. He has created the Universe so that all souls can explore and experience it in all its magnificence. He has given these souls this space in which to create, placing His energy equally in each soul. With that energy comes the precious gift of free will. It is this birthright that permits every soul to be the Creator of their life and their Destiny. There is no more powerful energy in the Universe than the power to create, for this power connects you to the Source from which you came.

Eons ago, a very large group of souls chose to incarnate and exist in the physical plane, which is the lowest level of vibration. By "lowest" I do not mean this Earthly experience is inferior to any other. It is not. Rather, it is the lowest level of vibration in terms of density. Just as a bass violin has a lower acoustical vibration than a flute, one is not a better instrument than the other. They simply vibrate at different frequencies. With excitement and curiosity, this large group of souls called themselves Humanity. They chose to go through a series of incarnations throughout time in order to experience cause and effect, balance, and the natural evolution of life in the physical world. Every person on this Earth belongs to that group of souls who came here using their free will to create and evolve. We are literally a group of Oneness that, for the time being, have separated into individual souls in order to experience the physical existence.

I tell you this, Dear One, to help you understand something very important. You are not here living as a human because you were cast out of anything, or because something bad happened. You are here because long ago I chose to be a part of this large group of souls and have the physical experience. As your soul, I have set forth the plan from which we are now living. I am the writer of this play and have set the stage. I have been given the choice to do so through free will. The Creator has formulated the blueprint we are to follow; *how* we follow it is up to each and every soul. God will not rescind or interfere with any soul's free will choices. Therefore, it is not God's Will that chooses who will die, who will suffer, and who will prosper. It is the soul's free will choice that determines those circumstances. It *is* God's Will that we remember we are One with Him so that we can recall while in physical form that we are Divine Beings who have the ability to create our lives and the capability to transform our lives through love.

I know that this is not an easy concept to understand. And it can be a troublesome notion for many, since it requires the belief that a soul and its human personality are responsible for the life they create together. This is a notion many people would rather dismiss because the human mind cannot fathom how it would choose any potentially negative life circumstance. Therefore, it is far easier to believe that God's Will must be responsible for what is happening in our lives and in our world.

The wonderful irony of it all, Dear One, is that since every soul *is* the Divine Presence of God, it *does* make God in charge of everything, but not in the sense of God as the overseer or judge. Instead, it is you using your free will to create how you are going to evolve in each lifetime. In that way, God *is* playing a part in what is happening in your life and in the world, because you are all God in full force.

Since I carry the remembrance that what God wants for Me is what I want for Me, I am God's Will determining how I want to create My lifetimes. Out of the Creator's love for Me, I have been given the free will to do so with every journey I have ever taken or will ever embark on. And even though some free will choices may take detours along the way, every detour teaches something that will enhance My evolvement. And since it is Me, the God in you, that carries the remembrance of why I am here, it is up to Me to influence you, My human counterpart, to follow the plan I have set forth. Every human being feels the nudging of its soul throughout the lifetime, even though it is not usually recognized as such. So, although I will nudge you to find your "calling" and steer you in the right direction, it is you who will choose to follow those "callings" or not.

This, Dear One, is your free will. You see, I have used My free will to determine My purpose for being here, but it is your free will as My human personality that will decide whether or not that purpose is served. This is why our life together is a co-creation. I determine the plan, and you make the choices in life that will make it happen or not. So, you see, God is in charge of your life, not as a force outside of you controlling your life, but as the Divine Presence within you helping you to awaken to your true potential as the Creator of your life.

I want you to remember, Dear One, that there is always a bigger picture that you cannot see with your human eyes going on in your life and in the world. For now, suffice it to say that, to help you truly understand My message, this will be explained more fully in the next letters. The Creator knows that all of us will find our way up the evolutionary spiral. It is part of the plan. The Grand Design has been forged with no strings attached. I have forever to make the right choices to evolve in My own Way, at My own pace, and in My own time. This, Dear One, is a most precious gift given to all of us from a most precious Love.

Formulating Your Own Destiny

Dear One,

In your everyday life, there is a plan so Divine that, if you remembered it, you would know that you are not here by accident. Like every other human being, you have a purpose for being here. Because I have been given the gift of free will, I am permitted to orchestrate what that purpose will be in each of My lifetimes. Every soul comes to the physical plane to fulfill a purpose, and it is through its human personality that a soul gets to work out what it came here to do. Before I entered the Earth plane, I knew there would be challenges and lessons awaiting me. I knew this because I could choose them ahead of time. The lessons I speak of are those of karma and soul growth. In this letter, I will specifically address the concept of karma because it is important to understand that karma is instrumental to the evolution of every soul.

Although in your physical world karma is viewed as a means to rectify misdeeds in past lives, it is much more than that. While Humanity tends to define karma as a negative or difficult life situation that is more of a punishment than a teaching tool, karma is anything but that. Quite simply, it is the spiritual law of cause and effect that says, "What you put out, you get back." When you pet an animal or tell someone you love him, you are creating a positive cause and effect. If you do things that bring joy into your life, or into the lives of others, you are creating positive karma that comes back to you. If you think, speak, or act in negative ways toward yourself

18

or others, you are creating negative karma. In other words, every cause has its effect, so whatever it is you create through thought, word, or deed, engenders a pattern that will return to you either in this lifetime or another.

I say this to you, Dear One, because many believe that karma is about an action taken against another. In essence, karma is more about the *mindset* underlying the action, rather than the action itself. For example, behind every act of jealousy lies the mindset of insecurity. Behind every judgment is the mindset of separation because you are forgetting that you and the one you are judging are One. The mindset of deprivation is behind every theft. It matters not whether the thief steals due to deprivation of food, or out of feeling deprived of love. Various mindsets cause everything one does. The purpose of karma is to understand those mindsets that were not understood during a previous lifetime so that the soul can come back and correct them in the present life.

You see, what gets created on the physical plane must also be corrected on the physical plane in order for the soul to achieve full realization of the lesson. In this way, it gives every soul the opportunity to face the unfinished business of correcting the previous mindset so the soul can have a new experience of it. This is why karma signifies balance, not punishment. In order to help them fully understand their past actions and how those actions have affected others, souls choose karma to correct a point in a past life that was out of balance. Each soul wants the chance to repair past consequences so it can move on to higher levels of creation with more opportunities for understanding. Remember, Dear One, there is always a higher place to go in terms of something else needing to be understood by the soul. In this way, repaying a karmic debt in a lifetime is an act of love, not a reprimand.

The difficulty in understanding karma is that you can never know what is karmic and what is not, and it is not important that you do know. How you react to a karmic situation is much more important than the life situation itself, for how you face your karma will determine your success in erasing it. Some souls choose a lifetime of very difficult lessons in order to eradicate a large debt in their karmic warehouse. They do this in order to escalate their evolution. These grievous karmic situations give them the opportunity to find unknown inner strengths that can become catalysts for change and growth. Not all souls choose such ambitious lessons, and it is all right. Every soul knows what is best for its evolution.

You will hear me say to you many times throughout these letters that you can never know the agenda of another's soul. What may appear tragic on the human plane is not tragic to the soul, for the soul remembers it has eternal life, and there is nothing more important to any soul than its growth. How that growth is experienced will be determined by every soul in its own way. Some lessons in life come more than once because they need to in order to be fully understood. Others come only once and are done. But whatever the lesson, you will need to be tested to see if you have learned the material. You cannot truly learn to master the art of driving and give yourself the freedom of movement in the world if you've only tested your driving skills in a parking lot.

Karma, then, is a stepping stone to growth because it is the soul's way of balancing its creations so it can continue to evolve. It is the soul's way of tying up loose ends and learning from the past while moving forward with the lesson learned. Karma can come in the form of a onetime incident, a mindset that has pervaded many lifetimes, or a relationship with another soul that needs balancing. Some karma can take many lifetimes to understand, while others can be fulfilled in an instant. How you answer to karma does not have to be manifested in a negative experience. For example, if you have been unkind to children in the past, you may decide to work with children in a gentle, loving way. A person who has abused another may come back as a counselor who helps those who have been abused. The outcome will always be for the greater benefit of the soul. This is why it helps to remember that a bigger picture exists in everyone's life. If you can see this as part of the plan, it will help you to remember that everyone is a soul first and a human second.

In this lifetime, I chose to address a karmic relationship with your mother. Actually, she chose Me by asking if I would participate in this lifetime with her in order to erase our karma from a past life. I agreed. You see, Dear One, on the spiritual plane, there is only love. As souls we remember our Oneness, which is why there are no resentments to hold us back from wanting to encourage and aid in another soul's growth. I knew that our relationship as mother and child would benefit both of us. I also knew that it would not be an easy one. Even though our free will brought us together to obliterate the karma between us, this, in itself, did not guarantee our success. Let me explain. Your mother succeeded in erasing her karma in this lifetime because she placed herself in a position that would require sacrifice on her part in order to take care of you, which she had not done in a previous life. The struggle she went through in order to do that was what was needed in order to successfully fulfill her karmic purpose. On the other hand, your hard-won karma was to forgive her. If you had not accepted or forgiven her, your karma would not have been fulfilled. For even though a soul determines its karma and purpose, it is the soul's human self that will or will not cooperate in completing them. Remember, Dear One, not only do I have free will, but you do, as well. For example, I can nudge you to follow the path of forgiveness, and you may know this is what you "should" do. Yet, you have the free will to decide whether or not to forgive. In this case, it took you many years to do so, but eventually you did. There are many who choose otherwise, and this is not a bad thing. It just means that the karma will be repeated in another life. So even though your relationship with your mother was not the fairy tale you hoped it would be, it did have a good ending.

This is why the agenda a soul puts forth must be determined before inhabiting the Earthly life. Souls know full well that, once they come into physical form, they will be too blind to have made the right choices for themselves. This is the difference between your Divine nature and your human one. Human nature says, "I would never have chosen this parent. I would never have chosen physical afflictions. I would never have chosen to be poor. I would never have chosen to be an alcoholic. I would never have chosen to live in this part of the world, and I would never have chosen to struggle." From a human standpoint, that is absolutely true. Because of its inability to know love in its purest form, the egocentric nature of the human being never would have made these choices, which is why your Divine nature, your soul, makes such decisions ahead of time. As souls, we are not concerned with what is comfortable or what is not; we are only concerned with what is going to help us get to where we want to go. I speak to you of karma in great length, Dear One, so you may understand life in a much different way and realize that there is much more going on than meets the eye.

As you know, I have nudged, poked, and prodded you throughout your life to follow the path of knowing yourself on a deep level. I have done so to help you discover your own underlying mindsets that create in this life your karma of joy or of suffering. There is something else, however, you must know about karma. Karma is not only a thing of the past. It is an ongoing occurrence in your everyday life. You create it on a daily basis by how you think, feel, and act. However, when you take the step of knowing yourself on a deeper level, you have the opportunity to realize that you are a Divine being who has a higher level of consciousness. And when you are able to remember this awareness, you will no longer make the same mistakes and continue to create the same karma. And if by chance you do make mistakes, you know that you have the spiritual awareness to rectify them right away. This, then, is the beginning of the end of your karma, and this, Dear One, is a big chunk of what the journey is all about.

As your soul, I am on the path of remembering so that one day I will choose not to return. I have come into a physical body as you, in order to create a destiny that will propel Me forward to higher levels of creation. Through the process of living many lives, I have taken the Light of Me, My Oneness with the Source of all Creation, and have allowed that Light to expand so that I may become a wiser and more fulfilled being.

It is with great love that I say to you, Dear One, do not look at your life as a problem to be solved, rather as an opportunity to re-member the lessons it can teach you. See it as the path of joy it really is, and embrace every situation with the remembrance that you are never given anything you can't handle.

No matter what appears to be insurmountable, you have brought with you everything you need to deal with it. You did not come into this lifetime without the right cards to play the right game.

Never forget, Dear One, that you have been given the Divine Power to achieve any purpose because you are a Divine Being living an everlasting Divine Life.

Soul Growth

Dear One,

Long before our first incarnation, those of us who chose the path of Humanity were totally aware that this journey would be an evolutionary process. We knew that returning to the physical plane throughout the Ages would be integral to that process. We knew we would be entering into a world of duality where both positive and negative outcomes are possible, depending upon choices made through our free will. Since up to that point our existence was based purely on love and Oneness, we had not yet experienced negativity. Therefore, we also knew that coming into a world of positive and negative energies would give us the opportunity to experience creation in a new and different way. With that said, it was understood that our spiritual evolution, as well as our evolution as a species, would be ongoing, so we awaited the journey with great anticipation. You see, Dear One, to think of spending thousands of years forgetting, remembering, and then rediscovering yourself as a Creator is an exciting notion for any soul. It is why I "bought the ticket for this ride" long ago. I wanted to play the Earthly "game of life."

I knew that participating in this game of life would entail answering to spiritual laws, one being the law of cause and effect. I had the complete knowledge that the underlying purpose of incarnation would be to remember Myself as a Divine Being. I also knew that I would experience lessons of soul growth that would support the act of remembering. I will explain. Soul growth is not exactly what it sounds like. It is not teaching the soul something new for its growth. Soul growth is putting into practice what the soul already knows and using it in the human life as a means for remembering. It differs from karma in that it is not a specific creation you erase from your slate. Instead, souls will look at their past lives and determine where the human self may not have been strong enough in remembering the soulful self. The soul then chooses areas of growth that will enhance that remembrance. I will use My existence as an example to help clarify its meaning, as well as My intentions for our life together.

In My spiritual reality, Dear One, I am love and all its variations. It is My nature to be loving, patient, compassionate, and kind. I can be nothing else. Yet, for this current lifetime, I chose the soul growth lessons of self-love and patience. I did not need to learn them. I needed to *use* them. As I looked back at My Earthly patterns before coming here, it was evident there had been many lives where My human self placed more emphasis on others than on Myself. My human personality had a recurring tendency to worry more about what others thought than what I thought, thereby placing emphasis on pleasing others rather than caring for My own needs. In others words, I made others more valuable and important than Me. This frame of mind created a lack of belief in Myself which lessened My self-worth. I could not remember Myself as a soul because I was too invested in making sure others approved of who I was as a human. Because of this pattern, I knew first and foremost that I wanted to be born during this time period because, more than any other time in history, this era would recognize the importance of self-esteem. In this way, it would give Me the greatest opportunity to help My human personality remember its Divine nature. There are many in your world, Dear One, who chose this same soul growth lesson for this reason. It is why I have nudged you so strongly to go deeper within yourself throughout your life. It has been a lifelong whisper from Me to you, and it is why you have had and still have the inclination to do so while helping others do the same.

In choosing the area of self-esteem I knew that if I was to find it, it would first have to be missing, since one does not look for something unless it is lost. Therefore, I knew that by being born into your particular family, there would be bumps in the road that would lead to insecurities within My human self. In other words, the stage would be set for love of self to be overlooked. By placing Myself in this situation, I would encourage you throughout this life to find it. I could have chosen more ideal parents and therefore a less painful childhood, but then there would have been less incentive to follow the path I set forth. I knew that lacking self-esteem in the human life would give you the opportunity, as well as the impetus, drive, and motivation to seek it. You see, Dear One, this is how souls think when they are not Earthbound. It really is a beautiful thing, even though it may not always feel that way to the human self.

Therefore, the soul growth of self-love that I was asking for would come out of this imperfection. From My soulful perspective, I needed to choose less-than-ideal circumstances for My coming into this world. I also knew you would need patience to deal with the ongoing process of self-love, which is why I also chose it as a soul growth lesson. It is not easy to wait for the proper timing for something to occur. To this day, you sometimes still think this book should have been finished earlier, but it is not so. Everything happens in its right and perfect time. The more you trust in this Divine process and the more you trust you, the more you love you. So you see, Dear One, self-esteem and patience go hand in hand, which is why you needed the influence of both.

Life will always be the initiator of soul growth because learning from one's soul is a constantly growing, forever process. Soul growth starts from the day you are born until the day you die. Everyone, whether in the state of remembering or not, is working on his or her soul growth. Everything in life is related to these lessons in order to enhance the remembering of who you are. You will know your soul growth by taking a closer look at your life and witnessing what continues to surface time after time. What areas of life are the most challenging? What lesson seems to keep repeating itself and, more important, how are you reacting to it? Do you make a change for the better, or do you remain stuck? When you find the courage to be honest, you will find what you came into this lifetime to remember. If you are willing to open your eyes, heart and mind, soul growth will make itself known. When one works on one's soul growth, the lesson diminishes and often completely disappears.

Although I have spoken to you in these last letters about the value of lessons, Dear One, know that I do not mean to give you the impression that souls are here only for these lessons. This is just part of the journey. I also came to this Earth anticipating tremendous love and joy. I looked forward to reunions with other souls who were with Me in other lifetimes who would join Me once again in My play. I relished the opportunity to enjoy the Earth and its beauty, and I was delighted at the prospect of using My creative abilities in all areas of My life.

Understand, Dear One, that although life may be a schoolroom, it is not a life sentence. It is a privilege. If you can view karma and soul growth as stepping stones toward a soul's evolution, you will gain a broader understanding of the bigger picture. There have been times when you have wondered why your life seems to be "blessed," while others suffer more than you. I tell you this: There is no life that is not blessed. God does not play favorites. Every human life has been determined by its soul for all the right reasons. I may have chosen a more "comfortable" life this time around in some respects, but it has not always been so. This life has also known painful lessons, discomfort, and challenges. Therefore, try not to compare your life to that of another. Instead, bless all those who have difficulty and, since you cannot know the agenda of another's soul, remember that soul growth occurs in every life. Perfection is born out of imperfection, which is the consummate unfolding of a soul's growth. Therefore, bless everyone, including yourself, for you are not here to measure whose life is painful or blessed, and whose is not. Allow everyone their own experience while you have yours.

Give yourself permission to embrace this incredible world for what it is, the greatest opportunity to evolve in the most effective way possible. Although you may not like everything you see, try to love it all, for nothing is going wrong in the Divine Plan of The One.

You Are Never Alone

Dear One,

How you loved to sit and play by yourself when you were small. From time to time, you would suddenly stop playing and look around the room as if someone was there. You would even stare into space, waiting for something to appear. Nothing did, but you sensed that you were not alone in the room. You were not frightened, just curious. Then, as if it was your imagination, you would return to your play. I am here to tell you, Dear One, it was not your imagination. You have never been alone. From the moment you came into this world, you have been surrounded by three invisible beings that have never left your side. They are your Spirit Guides. Unbeknownst to you, the child who suddenly stopped playing and stared into space was intuitively feeling the presence of her best friends.

After I made My choices of karma and soul growth for this lifetime, I knew there was one decision that was *not* going to be Mine to make, and that was who was coming with Me. I was assigned three incredible Guides for this journey. These Spirit Guides have been with Me since birth and will escort Me Home safely when this lifetime is over. They will never leave My side and they are here to assist no one else but Me. They are yours and Mine for life, here to support and serve us in the plan I have set forth. As I speak, one is standing behind you and the others are on either side of you, watching and reveling in this magnificent process. If you could feel them the way I do, they would seem like old friends coming back into your life.

Spirit Guides are no strangers to the Earthly plane. They differ from angelic beings in that they have experienced previous Earthly incarnations, whereas angels have not. Spirit Guides are completely aware of the trials, tribulations, and rewards of Earthly life and all that comes with it. They are teachers who have reached a level of evolution in which reincarnation is no longer necessary, because they have learned the lessons of Earth. It is My greatest desire to reach the level of a Spirit Guide; then I will know I have mastered the Earth plane.

All human beings have Spirit Guides who enter the lifetime with them. These Guides are chosen and matched according to the agenda of the soul to whom they are assigned. In other words, their assignment is not random. Every Spirit Guide has its own "expertise" gained from its own physical lifetime. In knowing My purpose, My Spirit Guides were assigned to Me based on their own particular abilities, to help Me fulfill what I set out to do. This makes communication between us easier because our energy packages are similar. Each Spirit Guide is especially selected to address your needs according to its mastery of the purpose you have chosen to fulfill. Although they work together as a team for your benefit, there are times when each dedicates its individual knowledge and proficiency to working with you on a separate area of your life.

The single function of all Spirit Guides is to help the soul fulfill its purpose. Your Spirit Guides are like a wreath wrapped around you that protects, loves, and serves you in any way you need. Many times this service takes the form of summoning other invisible forces to come to you when you need more than their assistance. This can be anything from asking writers to come to you while you write, healers to come when you are sick, or other loving spirits to come when you are fearful. Spirit Guides are able to summon anyone from the Universal Consciousness to be with you for certain amounts of time to engage in whatever you are trying to accomplish. They have the power to bring whatever you need from the Universe. This is why, Dear One, like Me, they really are your best friends.

Your Spirit Guides know that you are the master of your ship. They can in no way possess you. They are in the realm of God to guide and assist. Because you have your own free will, they are not here to coerce or tell you what to do. But they can help you find a way to know what you are supposed to do. Sometimes it can mean opening doors for you along the way, or they can come to you in the dream state so that when you awaken you may have a hunch, a feeling, or an idea about something. Spirit Guides can also come through you when you meditate. And like Me, they come to you most often through your intuition. They work by osmosis, Dear One, so the more time you take to be still, without the chatter of mind, the more you will have the opportunity to feel them. They are perpetually working for you through methods you would not even understand, and they are always with you. If for the moment you decide to shut them out, it will not detract from what they are here to do for you, and they will not go away.

It is important for you to know that the relationship with your Spirit Guides is not one-sided. You give back to them by giving them the opportunity to help you achieve what you have come here to do. And if you do not achieve what you had hoped for, it makes no difference. Your Spirit Guides know you will continue to learn through soul growth and that they will continue to evolve on the ethereal plane as your mentors. You must realize, Dear One, that by being with you in this adventure, they are not only attaining spiritual growth, they are also experiencing another point in time with new energies, new experiences, new languages, new cultures, and most of all, new understandings. Since they learn by observation, you are teaching them, as well as receiving their teachings.

31

Your particular Guides are quite pleased to be a part of this book, so I shall reintroduce them to you and tell you of the love they have for you. The one that stands directly behind you is Camille. She is the absolute energy of peace, a gentle energy, an energy of light that goes to you and through you. Her light adds to yours so you may also give light to others. When you sing, she rides on the vibrations that come forth because it brings her great joy. She gives you the ability to dream and imagine, and to inspire and create. She helps you stop worrying, and is here to remind you that, even on the darkest day, there is always light. She brings effervescence into your world when it seems to be going flat. When you were a child, she often talked to you. You didn't know what it was, but you liked it. If there is a need for solace, she will come and walk with you at night in the astral plane to comfort you. She helps ease the energy within you and leaves you feeling rested, so that when you awaken, you feel clearer. This is her job. She is a joyous light, exuberant about life, which is why your energies match so well. You surf this exuberance together. Think of Camille as a lovely pot of soup on a low simmer, putting forth the most delicious aroma that makes you want more of it. She helps heal you, Dear One, like a delicious pot of soup.

The Spirit Guide to your left is called Remet. He has come into your life to be your stabilizer. He is like the rudder of a ship that keeps it steadfast. He reminds you that balance is important. More than any of the other Guides, he encourages you to play and sees your need for it more than you do. He inspires you at times to put your feet up and do nothing so you can truly accept yourself. Remet knows that, because you have come into this life with an agenda for serving others, you have a tendency to overwork. Sometimes you burn the candle at both ends trying to get everything accomplished. So he protects you by reminding you not to overdo it and to rest.

Remet often whispers to you that it is okay for you to want the best. He loves it when you hum because he, too, resonates beautifully with music. He also brings you the ability to take the second look that will help get you to the middle road of an issue, which is not necessarily a lesser road, but usually a safer one. In his past life he was a fine writer, so he easily reaches you through words and helps bring the energy and power of words to their true balance within you to enrich your own writing. You are his pride and joy, Dear One. He sees you as a magician who gives shape to the lives of others, and he helps you to heal them and yourself.

Always standing tall at the right side of your body is your American Indian of the Cherokee nation. He is called, Singing Wind. He comes to remind you that you are the wind, the water, the fire, and the Earth, for he knows that your Spirit has no boundaries. He whispers to you, "Let yourself be the air, to float and soar. Let yourself be the water and feel its calming coolness. Feel the heart and spirit of fire. Know that all this is one with the solid strength of Earth." He tells you that, to swim with the fish and soar with the eagle, you must learn to let go.

At dawn, when the world begins to come alive and sing, he sends his energy to you. When you first awaken, you do not want anything or anyone to intrude upon your sense of peace, quiet, and commitment to yourself. This is the energy of Singing Wind speaking to you. In a sense, it is as though you are being cradled in his calm and peaceful energy. A tremendous sense of appreciation for yourself and your life comes from your heart into your mind. Singing Wind gives you this gift of the morning, Dear One. And he also brings you receptivity to Nature, for Nature heals. He opens your eyes to see that what lives in Nature is not separate from you, but is there to assist you to be a better version of who you are. For she who can appreciate the beauty of a blossom, will blossom inside herself. As a highly evolved soul, Singing Wind chose to be your connection to the Universe through the energy of Nature, knowing that it is now more essential than ever for people to reunite with the natural world.

He wants you to know that the tree, no matter how battered, can bud and bloom again if its roots go deeper and make it strong. He reminds you that this is who you are.

Dear One, throughout the years your three Spirit Guides have helped you have faith in yourself. This wonderful triad has been your support system for the smallest to the largest situations. They will help with nearly anything you need – from removing a pebble on your path, to shielding you from a furious storm. Although they are not here to answer *all* of your needs, they are here to open doors, so that you may progress. As you write this book, they are working with you on trust, helping you believe that talking with Me is not just a possibility, but a probability. Much of the time, they are quite nosy as they gather to look over your shoulder to admire your writing. Whether or not you do anything with the book, all three want you to write for the pure joy of it because that is the true author in you. They continue to send you messages that life is joyous, and meant to be lived in just that way.

There is nothing more gratifying for Spirit Guides than having their humans become aware of their existence. It is rare that they receive this acknowledgment. Most human beings do not know they are surrounded by entities who not only have been chosen for them, but who also care about them. Think of your Spirit Guides as friends in the unseen world and, just as you would reach out to a friend in the seen world, reach out to them. It delights them to be honored in this way. It thrills them even more to have their presence acknowledged, even if you do not know who they are. Just say hello. Like Me, they can hear your thoughts, so speak to them either aloud or silently, and let them in. And don't forget to ask them for help, for they are here to comfort, guide, and assist you in any way they can.

In the world I come from, everything (including Nature) has its own Spirit Guide to watch over it. There is nothing in God's Creation that is not guided or protected. Along with My Spirit

Guides, you and I have a Guardian Angel that not only watches over us, but also watches over them. Everyone does. Your Spirit Guides and Guardian Angel communicate with each other quite often. In fact, your Guardian Angel has a propensity to sit at the end of the bed while you sleep, just to be with you. I write these things to you, Dear One, because it is important for you to know that never in your life have you been alone, nor will you ever be alone. So, if you begin to feel that way, try to remember that you are always watched over and guided with love. God would have it no other way.

It has been My wish that these letters help you understand the process a soul experiences before coming into Earthly life, so that you may recognize your true identity of being a soul first and a human second. Try not to view yourself as a human being walking around with a soul. Instead, visualize yourself as a soul walking around as a human being. This actually can make a big difference in how you view your life and the world.

Up to this point, I have explained to you how and why I chose the purpose of this lifetime. Once I was given My spiritual supporters to guide Me, there was one more very important decision I had to make before being allowed entrance to the Earth plane and on to My next adventure. It was time for Me to choose the human personality I would use in this physical lifetime. In other words, Dear One, it was time for Me to adopt you.

Awaiting the Heavens

Dear One,

You are One with everyone and everything. Although you may not think of yourself as being One with a flower, a rock, a bug, and at times a fellow human being – you are indeed One with all of them. It is not possible for you to be anything else, for God is in everyone and everything. You could say that each of you on this Earth, along with every flower, rock, and bug, carry the vibrational DNA of the Creator. Everything in the Universe has its own consciousness and is made from the energy of God. The reason I say this to you is because it is time for me to speak of the last decision I had to make before I was permitted entrance into the physical plane. To help you understand this, you must know that your Oneness with everything is part of that decision. This not only pertains to the Earth, but also to everything in the Universe, including its solar system. Therefore, not only are you connected in mind, body, and spirit while living a physical life, you are connected to the Sun, Moon, planets and stars, as well. In fact, the planets and their positions in the sky affect the cyclic patterns of your individual lives, your countries, and your world, just as they affect the cyclic occurrences of oceans and weather patterns. The astrological vibrations of the solar system affect everyone and everything. It is this very solar system that provided Me with the emotional structure of the human personality I was to become. In other words, Dear One, the positions of the planets at the time of your birth were paramount in My choosing you.

Once I decided to work on a relationship from My karmic warehouse, having chosen the soul growth areas of self-esteem and patience and having been given the right and perfect Spirit Guides to assist Me in this purpose, I then chose the time period of My birth. This is one of the most important decisions a soul makes before incarnating, for it is the human personality that will acclimate and aid the soul in its purpose throughout an entire lifetime, no matter how long that may be. Therefore, the "energy package" of the human personality I choose for a particular lifetime is vitally important, because the time of My birth will determine the inherent nature of who that human personality will be.

If you have your astrological natal chart interpreted by a reputable astrologer, you would find that each sign of the zodiac has a particular core personality with associated key words and qualities. Therefore, you are not just your Sun sign as seen in a newspaper column. You are also a compilation of eleven other influencing planets that dwell in the twelve houses of the life chart. By viewing your own astrological natal chart, you can witness the blueprint I set forth for this lifetime and the energy package I chose in order to fulfill My purpose. So, Dear One, although I have had no say in your genetics, I do play a great part in how you see things, how you react, and how you use your strengths and weaknesses.

The time period of My birth determined the characteristics of My human personality, and the personality I chose was based on the soul growth I asked for. Consequently, I waited for the configuration of the heavens to present Me with the emotional structure of you, My human personality, to help Me encounter and encompass these soul growth areas. Because I chose the soul growth areas of self-love and patience, I knew I would need the qualities of determination, commitment, perseverance, and a strong will – for these qualities would help My human personality to "stay the course." To have the desire and dedication to plunge into the deeper levels of the psyche is not an easy task for a human being. Knowing that I was charting a difficult course, I needed a personality with the ability to endure the process of fulfilling My purpose. I also needed that personality to have the drive, energy, enthusiasm, and motivation to keep this hard-working engine in balance and perfect alignment. In other words, I needed a personality with the innate quality to commit to a lifelong goal and, at the same time, have the stamina to maintain that commitment. It was then, Dear One, that I knew that the ideal energy package for My purposes would be for you to be born a Capricorn.

If there is any sign that has its "eye-on-the-prize" and is driven to work toward a goal until success reigns supreme, it is the Capricorn personality. Born with a strong sense of responsibility and dedication, they are extremely hard-working and need to feel useful and effective to be satisfied with their lives. The Capricornian goat is tenacious like no other sign in that it will climb slowly and steadily up a steep mountain or rocky cliff until it reaches the top. Of all the signs of the zodiac, it is Capricorn who scales the highest peaks of all. This is why your particular natal chart illustrates that four of your twelve planets are in Capricorn, and all of them reside in the first house, which is the house of self-awareness. So, you see, Dear One, you were no accident. You were very much "on purpose." Knowing that I could have the characteristics of Capricorn together with fulfilling the karmic debt involving your mother, was absolutely perfect for Me. It doesn't always work out that way. In this case, it did.

At the time of your birth, the energy of Sagittarius also prevailed, giving you the needed qualities of enthusiasm, adventure, optimism, high energy, and the desire to search for truth and knowledge. You needed these qualities to balance the serious dedication of the goat. Thus, when the planets and stars aligned with this configuration, I knew that this particular "Cosmic toolkit" was the emotional structure I was looking for. Always remember, Dear One, that you are more than a by-product of your parents' biology and behavior. You are here in vibrational harmony with the Universe, which influences who you are in your everyday life. You are also here in this time-frame with your own soul's agenda and your own human personality to help you fulfill that agenda.

And so, with our agenda set for this lifetime and the configuration of the heavens in place to support My mission, I was ready for this journey. It was time for Me to live in two dimensions at once and enter the Earthly illusion of forgetting, so that we could have the opportunity to remember. Consequently, three days after Christmas in the year 1948, you and I came into this life together.

Amnesia Is Part of the Plan

Dear One,

When you were a newborn you remembered Me totally. All babies do at first. They may not be able to communicate or control their bodies, but they are very aware beings fresh from "Heaven." You had this remembrance for many years until you began to grow into your childhood. By the time you were four years old, the "forgetting" began, and by the age of seven you had forgotten you were Me. You need to know that this is not a bad thing. I knew you would gradually detach yourself from the remembrance of Me so you could fit into the physical world. Amnesia is necessary for every human being, because one must learn and adjust to being human while living on Earth. One must learn to walk, run, ride a bike, hold a pencil, put on clothes, read, follow rules, and socialize with others. It is part of the human process. Therefore, the amnesia is really a detachment from Me that fully directs your energies to learning the physical needs of being human. It is supposed to be this way.

This is the course, Dear One, which all children go through. They need to become completely identified with the human part of themselves and forget what they came back to Earth to achieve. In order to live a human life, you must learn about being a human, which means living the life of one who has forgotten, at least for the time being. If in your human form you already had the remembrance, there would be no growth. You need to forget in order to make the plan work. If you remembered everything when you got here, there

40

would be no way to determine whether you learned the lesson you set forth to experience. This is why your memory is taken away.

Giving you the answers to your own exam would be too easy. You would experience no development or growth. This would be like a person who goes to college to become a teacher, studies hard, earns good grades, but never goes into a classroom. While this student really wants to be good at teaching, he or she will never know whether that can happen. Knowledge without experience is not enough. One becomes a good teacher through experience gained in the classroom, by seeing what makes a good teacher and learning what one needs to remember to be that kind of a teacher. There has never been a first-year teacher who knew it all. So it is with souls. We, as well, evolve into being what we want to be through the classroom of life, through the struggle, the joys, the ups, downs, mistakes and successes. This is part of the deal when a soul decides to enter the Earth plane once again. If I came here with the full knowledge and realization of everything I wanted to accomplish, what kind of accomplishment would that be?

Therefore, we come into this physical existence as souls wearing the blinders given to us. The state of forgetting is a vital part of the Creator's plan. By forgetting, we are given the opportunity to remember. And so, Dear One, I know that as I enter the illusion of Earthly life once more, it is only one dream among many that I have had. You, as My human personality, will not know it as a dream. You will see and feel it as your reality. Like any dream that invades your sleep until you wake up and realize it was only a dream, it will feel real at the time.

So the best you can do with the illusion of life, Dear One, is to understand it and have as much power over it as you possibly can. You are here to live in this illusion for a very short while, but it cannot and will not have power over you unless you permit it. It is important to recognize the illusion for what it is, and not become addicted to it by thinking that this is all there is. To do this, you must try to remember that you are a part of a greater reality.

Once I knew you had forgotten who you are, Dear One, it was then that I began the nudging, the whispering, and the calling for you to awaken once more. My lifelong task is to help My Sleeping Beauty wake up. That awakening comes when you begin to realize that you and God are One. Since the majority of your world is still asleep in this way, the remaining letters in these next sections are to help you and your world awaken, so you can begin changing your life to remember and become the powerful Creator you are. These letters are the keys to opening the power within you, thereby giving you everything you have ever asked for and more. And as always, Dear One, they are sent with great love.

Section II:

Open These Letters When You Want to Remember How Life Really Works

If You Don't Live It, You Don't Know It

Dear One,

The purpose of writing these letters is to reveal My truths to you and to help you remember them. They are the roadmap that will help you become aware of yourself as a Divine Being living here in human form for a Divine purpose. These truths exist to show you the relationship between growing as a human and evolving as a soul. Acting on them will require great honesty and courage on your part, for when you are human, no matter how spiritual you are, there is always resistance. I say this to you because some of these letters may appear to be "too simple," so there may be a tendency to say to yourself, "Oh, I know this already." As soon as you have that thought, your ego has just entered the room and the resistance has begun. You will have closed the door within yourself and jeopardized your chances of knowing truth more deeply.

The ego of every human personality, Dear One, is a complex thing. In its positive state, it empowers and gives you the strength that assists you throughout your life. In its negative state, it is demeaning, fearful, and resistant to believing you are more than who you think you are. In this case, thinking you "already know something" comes from the negative part of the ego that wants you to believe that you are *above* thinking you could use what you already know to learn something new. In this way it keeps you from taking a closer look at yourself. I will explain this further in other letters, but for now, know that every human being has some resistance to experiencing his or her belief on the deepest possible level, which is to live it. This is not a bad thing. It comes with the territory of being human. It is important, however, to keep an eye on that part of you that may want to skip over any letter you think is common knowledge or something you think you already know. If you are not living what it is you say you know, then you do not have the full realization of that belief.

There are truths in these letters that are simple in nature. Yet, the process of living these truths is not at all easy. Throughout time, many Masters have given us fundamental truths. How much simpler can it get than, "Do unto others as you would have them do unto you," or "Love thy neighbor as thyself?" These are simple truths. Yet, in your world, truths that are "believed" by millions of people are often not lived. If they were, the world would be a different place. Therefore, Dear One, do not let your approach to truth become an intellectual exercise. Instead, pay attention to what you truly believe and see if you are living it. If you are not, then truth only lives in your head, not in your heart.

For example, if you believe it is okay to make mistakes, yet you chastise yourself for making one, you really don't believe that it's okay to make them. If you say you forgive those who antagonize you, yet you still feel consistently angry with them, you believe in the concept of forgiveness rather than the reality of it. If you view yourself as a spiritual person who believes in Oneness, yet you spend time gossiping, you haven't learned a thing about Oneness. If you march in anti-war protests because you wish for world peace, but do not seek peace within yourself, then you know nothing of this truth. If "living in the moment" is an ideal you want to uphold, yet your time is spent dwelling in the past or the future, you are not living the truth you say you want to embrace. Therefore, one of the first steps in knowing yourself and living the life of a powerful Creator is to become aware of how unaware you can be about living your truth. Do you really live what you believe? It's as "simple" as that.

I say this to you out of love, Dear One, for it is My purpose to help you awaken and understand that truth is a way of life. It is a living, breathing part of you. It is not something that only requires belief. It is something you live. You can have all the awareness in the world, but if you aren't applying it by living it, it means nothing. Anyone can be a perpetual student and have a long checklist of all they have learned. But if you aren't using it in your everyday life, then it has no real value. Once you start living the checklist, however, you will grow and become an essential part of a world that needs you.

And so, regarding any letter you come upon in this book, do not think, "I know this already." Instead, look beyond the words. Go deeply into the words and into your heart to find the courage to see yourself clearly. As you read these letters ask yourself, "Is this a truth I believe in? If so, do I live it or do I not? If not, what keeps me from doing so?" These are some of life's difficult questions, but they are necessary if you want to follow the path of a spiritual seeker.

Do not be afraid to know the deepest truths, Dear One. You are here to live them. You are quite capable of this, and you must not be afraid to attempt it. Everyone has the capability to live their truth, but few accept the challenge. Be one that does. Live your truth, no matter what it is, for in so doing will you find your way back to Me, the truest part of you.

Life Is an Inside Job

Dear One,

You are timeless. If you ponder these three words for a moment, imagining what it would be like if you truly believed you were a timeless being, you may begin to feel a stirring within. It would be similar to the sensation a mother has when she first feels life in her womb. When you feel this eternal truth, even slightly, you begin to remember that you are not just a participant in life. You are Life itself. You are the timeless Me inside of you. I start this letter with these three words because I am here to talk to you about life, not just the human story of you throughout the years, but the realization that you have everything it takes to create life the way you want it to be because you are the energy of Life itself.

As you know, the plan I set forth before coming here affects the life we are in. Lessons of soul growth and karma enter as opportunities for us to experience. As My partner in life, you also have the ability to create the situations of this lifetime because life is a cocreation between a soul and its human personality. This means that you are in a partnership with God and have been partnering with God since He created you. This partnering is called, "your life."

If you are not aware of how life is created, then life will seem random and, at times, unfair. This is why I have devoted a section of this book to life and how it is created by you and Me, so that you can understand how you play a crucial part in what transpires.

Always remember, Dear One, that life is not separate from you. It does not have a power of its own. Contrary to popular belief, it does not randomly hand out lemons so you can make lemonade. It is neither a bowl of cherries, nor is it a bitch and then you die, according to your common vernacular. Life doesn't happen in spite of you. Life happens *because* of you. So when you ask yourself, "I wonder what life is going to bring me?" or "I wonder where life is going to take me?" you are expressing a belief that life is something outside of you over which you have no control. Nothing could be farther from the truth. Since you carry within you the Consciousness of All That Is and Ever Was, it is impossible for anything, especially your life, to be separate from you. You were made in the image and likeness of God, which means you are a Creator. You did not come here to inhabit a body and do nothing. You came here to create, and your life is the result of that creation.

Most people in this world have not yet recognized that all things happen from the inside out. Know, Dear One, that there is always a direct correlation between the inner world of what you think, feel, and believe and what is showing up in your outer world. This is how creation works and how it affects your individual life. I will take this one step further and tell you that the accumulation of every human being's inner life is what creates the state of the world. This is how powerful Humanity is.

There is still much resistance to this truth, however, because believing that you are the Creator of your life is a frightening prospect for many people. Some are afraid of what they would do with that kind of power, even though the thought of it may appeal to them. Others do not like the idea of believing that they create their lives because it would mean having to take responsibility for it. Then there would be no one to blame for how their life turns out. But what if people truly believed there *is* a connection between disease and "dis-ease?" What if they knew firsthand that their relationship problems could be the result of their own fears of intimacy? What if they took off their blinders and discovered that the inner stories they tell about themselves affect every aspect of their lives – from their finances, the state of their health, and how they are treated, to how happy or unhappy they are? For the most part, your world is still asleep when it comes to this manner of thinking because it is less threatening for people to believe that life is a nebulous entity dispersing havoc or blessings at will than it is to think that they have had a hand in creating it.

I agree, Dear One, that it is not easy to think that you have attracted your life circumstances as part of creating your life. It takes a courageous and honest person to even begin to fathom this concept. The reality is, however, that life is not a haphazard series of random coincidences. You are where you are in life as a direct result of your own thinking process. Not only is your course charted by Me and the plan I set forth for this journey, but it is created also by you. I can tell you who you are, and where you came from, but this will mean nothing to you unless you know how to create your life once you get here. The remaining letters are written to help light the way.

Life is truly an inside job. Every answer you've ever looked for already resides within you. You hold the key to your own remembering. You have the ability to unlock the door of your own unhappiness, worry, doubt, and fear. When you look inside yourself to understand who you are, you will realize the power you have, not only to create your life, but also to experience the joy of playing with life. And life is meant to be played with, Dear One. It isn't a problem to be solved. It is to be lived. You have the power of the Universal God Mind within you which can alter any situation, as long as you trust and believe in it. When you do so, you can take life anywhere you want to go. If I can help you understand that God is your Source of all supply, and that this abundance lives within you, you will see how effortless and enjoyable life can really be.

There is no greater opportunity for you than to be here experiencing the Divine miracle of starring in this illustrious play you call "life." The supporting players are lined up and the so-called villains are ready to aggravate you and give you the opportunity to move beyond them. The heroes are on stage at the right and perfect time you need them to be. You have invited them all into your play. You are Divine Life starring in your Earthly play of life, where you will encounter many life situations. Even then, Dear One, understand that you are not limited solely to the situation of this current life. You have been an eternal soul experiencing many life situations in order to be Life itself. Your life is God experiencing Himself through you and your creations. So the curtain goes up, the lights go on, and you have the incredible opportunity to be the star of your life with the ability to shape your character's journey. And since the greatest creation of your existence is always going to be "your life," know that you are the ultimate Creator of it. Don't be afraid, Dear One. Instead, revel in the miracle of it, rejoice in this incredible gift, and know that I am always with you to help you along the way.

Energy Follows Thought

Dear One,

Before I entered the density of the physical life, I lived in the world I call Home, the ethereal world of Spirit. It is the invisible world that surrounds this one, although you cannot see it with the human eye. You will remember it instantly, however, when you leave this world. It is where creation takes place on many levels and where Mankind brings forth ideas to be manifested on the physical plane. Nothing exists in your world that has not begun as a thought in the spiritual realm. I tell you this because it is imperative that you understand that the power to create your life comes from your Divine ability to create through the vehicle of thought.

As an evolving soul, when I am not in a lifetime on Earth, I continue to create by determining whatever it is I desire. For example, if I want to be in the presence of someone here on the spiritual plane, or even someone on the Earth plane, all I have to do is think of them and I am by his or her side. If My wish is to sit by a beautiful waterfall and feel Oneness with the glorious energy of that setting, all I have to do is think about being there, and I am immediately transported to that place. If I want to learn about something – whether it is for the pure joy of it (such as music or another art), or whether I want to bring a talent or a particular teaching back to the physical plane for My next life – I am instantly in the setting where that learning will take place. Yes, Dear One, in the spiritual realm souls continue to learn and grow on every imaginable level, for this is the birthplace of all knowledge and wisdom.

Therefore, when I came into this world of physical form, I brought with Me the power of thought, which is the foundation of all creation. Other than love, no greater force resides within you. What you think on a consistent basis will create what will occur in your life. It can be no other way. This is how creation works, whether you are in the spiritual realm or whether you live on the physical plane. The only difference is that in the spiritual realm thoughts are instantly manifested. On the physical plane this takes longer because of the Earth's density.

In your human existence, there are only two kinds of energy: positive and negative. Therefore, there are only two kinds of thoughts, positive and negative. When you give birth to a thought, other thoughts of a similar nature vibrate with that thought and create more like it. When one negative thought attracts another negative thought, which together attract even more negative thoughts, before you know it you can find yourself depressed, not realizing that the depression was caused by what you were just thinking. Consequently, your thoughts project either positive or negative energy into the Universe, which thereby attracts similar energy back to you.

Energy follows thought, Dear One. Whatever you are thinking has a force of energy behind it that is creating what comes back to you, thereby affecting your life. Never underestimate the impact of thoughts. They are not little wisps of static floating around in the air with no meaning. They are powerful snippets of God letting loose whatever it is you are thinking about and bringing back to you what you have just sent. Remember, Dear One, you are always a vibrational being first and a physical being second.

You could say that thoughts are like planted seeds. If you plant virtual dandelion seeds and water them often with negative thoughts, weeds are going to spring up in your garden of life. These "weeds" can manifest themselves as emotional upsets, health problems, financial troubles, or relationship issues. Therefore, what you think is life altering. In essence, you are largely the result of every repetitious thought you've ever had. So it really is the thought that counts.

If people were to pay closer attention to what they are thinking, they might be quite amazed to see that the majority of their everyday thoughts are mostly negative. They may think they are thinking in a positive manner, but closer examination will tell them differently. For example, if you want more love in your life, but continue to focus your thoughts on the love you are missing, the Universe can only send back what you are focusing on, which is not having enough love in your life. If you wish for financial abundance but are centered on thoughts of lack, abundance cannot come to you. Therefore, you cannot expect to receive what you want in life if you are thinking more about what you don't want.

It is important to understand that the Universe does not have an agenda of its own. It does not randomly bestow blessings or punishments, nor does it decide for you what is going to show up in your life. It is merely a mirror that reflects what you are thinking about on a consistent basis. So if you want to feel good physically, emotionally, or spiritually, and you are not getting your wish, it is because you are not thinking in a way that vibrationally matches what it is you say you want. There are no exceptions to this spiritual law. This is why it is so important to become aware of your thoughts. A heightened awareness level on your part will always help reinforce the belief that you, indeed, do play a definite role in what is showing up in your life.

Know, Dear One, that you can change anything you want to change that has to do with you. This is how powerful you are. The only thing that keeps you from having what you want is the thought that you can't have it. Positive thoughts will bring you positive results. Let your negative thoughts be the teacher that reminds you of what you do not want. The wonderful thing about negative thoughts is that they give you the desire to think something new. No matter how awful you think they are, they give you the opportunity to choose differently and propel yourself forward. Therefore, never demean yourself for having them. They are in your life for a good reason, and they are positive in that they help you to grow. They also help you to seek a better thought, which not only makes you feel better, but also guides you on the path of becoming a more conscious Creator of your life. If you can take your mind off automatic pilot and put it in manual mode where you start paying attention to what you are thinking, you will steer your plane effectively in the direction you want it to go. This is how you are the Creator of your life.

Throughout this book I will continue to talk about the virtue of thought, for it is the foundation of all creation. Everything that manifests in your world is a result of thought. As evidenced by your nightly news programs, millions of people are creating millions of negative thoughts every day. This is why it is so important to know that what you are thinking on a daily basis not only affects your life, but also affects the world you live in.

Your thoughts are your destiny, Dear One. If you plant the seeds of joyous, loving thoughts, your future garden will be filled with beautiful flowers, because what you think today creates what awaits you in your future. Let nothing hold you back from believing that you are worthy of having what you want. Stop once a day and take inventory of the kinds of thoughts you are sending out. All you have to do is take a moment to ask yourself if you are steering your plane in a positive or negative direction. I tell you this: if you are going to be picky about anything in your life, there is no better way to spend your time than being choosy about what you think. Remember what I said at the beginning of this letter. I have brought with Me the power of creation, which is thought. This means your inherent God nature enables you to create your heart's desire. Start believing in yourself as a magnificent Being of Light who can create whatever she wants, because that is *exactly* who you are.

Beliefs Create the Rules of Your Life

Dear One,

In My last letter, I encouraged you to pay attention to your thoughts. Now I will take this one step further. To more fully understand how you create your life, you need to understand the power of belief. A belief is much more than a thought. It is a thought that you have had many times to which you eventually become attached. Whether positive or negative, it is a thought you find difficult to let go of. The most prevailing kind of belief is an inner core belief which for the most part is deeply ingrained and extremely powerful. Most people have at least one core belief, and some have many. Because core beliefs are usually old and hidden, they often do not reside in the conscious awareness. They do, however, continue to create circumstances in life because they also carry the energy of thought. The only difference is that core beliefs are tucked away where you can't find them, unless you go looking.

The iceberg analogy is a good illustration. The visible tip of an iceberg in the ocean represents only one-tenth of its size. The remaining nine-tenths lie under the water. Therefore, the unseen part of the iceberg is by far larger than what is seen. So it is with human awareness. What you are not aware of within yourself is much greater than what you are aware of. And since you know only one-tenth of yourself because you identify solely with what is sticking out of the water, you can see why you are potentially blind to the totality of what you are creating in your life. It is not just the one-tenth of you that creates, Dear One. It is all of you.

Most people think that the tip of the iceberg is the reality of life, yet much of what makes them "tick" lies under the ocean. In actuality, your life gets created on three levels. As My human personality, you are creating from what you consciously and unconsciously put forth. I create, as well, by bringing areas of soul growth that need to be experienced into this lifetime. And so, you have three minds that are in the process of creating your life: your conscious mind, which is the tip of the iceberg, your unconscious mind, which is the iceberg under the ocean, and your Superconscious mind, which is Me, the ocean itself, that surrounds them all.

To find the buried treasure of hidden beliefs, you must look for them under the water. You must go to the place where these beliefs originated, a place from long ago, your childhood. The majority of core beliefs come from the child within who has had to make up these beliefs in order to cope with life. Although children have a tendency to inherit their parents' beliefs as well, they also have their own set of rules about who they are based on feelings they cannot understand. In general, children think that everything is about *them* because they do not have the cognitive ability yet to discern what is truth and what is not. Therefore, they feel responsible for what happens in the family and, in turn, make up beliefs about themselves in order to make sense of what is going on. All children do this to some degree, but some do it more than others. In either case, all children grow into adults who are unaware that they continue to embrace these outdated beliefs that no longer serve them.

I will use one of your core beliefs as an example, Dear One, to illustrate how this happened to you. When your parents separated during your childhood, it did not occur to you to think that your father left the marriage, or simply left your mother or brother. You felt that he left you and believed that if he really loved you, he would have stayed. As the months and years passed without his desire to see you regularly, you became convinced there must be something wrong with you. Thus, you formed the belief that you must be unlovable. You could not understand why a father would not want to see his child, especially a father you loved so much. While you do not consciously remember thinking repeatedly, "I am unlovable," you did think it and feel it over and over again, until this thought became a deeply imbedded belief. You made the *incorrect* assumption that if you were really lovable, he would have come back for you. You could not fathom that a weakness resided in him, so you wound up believing that the shortcoming was yours. After all, what little girl wants to think her Prince Charming is a dud. Hence, a core belief was formed from a thought you became attached to, the thought that something about you was unlovable. And that one belief, until discovered, caused a domino effect in your life for years. You are not alone in this boat, Dear One. Many people harbor similar core beliefs at the bottom of their emotional oceans.

As an aside, I want you to know something. Your father did love you. At that time in his life, however, he was just not capable of giving you what you needed because he could not give to himself what *he* needed. The blessing underneath all this is that his loss propelled you inward to discover the core beliefs that eventually led you to find love of self and to discover Me. And in time, you found each other again and filled your relationship with love.

Therefore, to say the least, there is tremendous energy in a core belief. When you touch upon even *one* in your life, you will have accomplished a major success in reaching the mother-lode of creation. What most people discover when they uncover a core belief is that their whole life has been spent believing something that is not true. I can tell you, and others can tell you, that there is nothing unlovable about you, but if you have not discovered and discarded this inner belief, it will not matter what anyone says. You will still believe your core belief until *you* decide to change it. However, since you uncovered this particular core belief years ago, you have made the unconscious part of you more visible. Because of that, more of your iceberg has surfaced to be seen. The tip of your iceberg changed from being one-tenth in size to four-tenths in size. This is the value of knowing yourself, Dear One. The more your awareness becomes heightened, the greater the probability you have of not making the same mistakes, thereby changing everything in your life for the better.

As you know, uncovering a core belief requires a willingness to look deeply within yourself. Only the most courageous take this plunge because it requires time, effort, honesty, and patience to break the old patterns of thinking. Becoming aware of what lies under the water is a venture worth taking. It is a necessary component for all those wanting to know themselves more fully in order to become a powerful Creator.

Although finding the unconscious part of you is not easy, it does not have to be laborious. You just need to go exploring. To take the first step, you must address any guilt, shame, or unlovable issues you are carrying around, for it is these kinds of negative feelings that long ago created beliefs of unworthiness and unlovability. And if you cannot think of any right away, ask your little one inside. She will know exactly what I'm talking about. Another path to finding your core beliefs is to listen to how you talk to yourself. What "truths" do you claim about who you are? What particular beliefs do you harbor that are "written in stone" about you? What names do you call yourself? Listen to the negative thoughts swirling around in your head because these are part of your core beliefs coming to the forefront so you can look at them and change them. The other way to uncover a core belief is to listen to how you think negatively about others. Most human beings do not realize that when they think or speak ill of someone, most often they are talking about the qualities that lie hidden within themselves. They transfer these traits to others so they don't have to see their own issues lying beneath the ocean.

Beliefs do create the rules of your life, Dear One. If you believe you're a clumsy person, you will trip. If you believe you're forgetful, you won't remember. If you believe all men are jerks, you will most likely end up with one. If you believe you do not deserve, you will not get what you want. If you believe you are stupid, you will act stupid. If you believe you are a loser, you will never win. The ensuing result of your beliefs is that what you believe will always become a self-fulfilling prophecy.

It is wonderful when one's core beliefs are positive. It is beautiful to behold anyone feeling worthy of whatever the world has to offer. There are both positive and negative core beliefs within you. It is the latter, however, that I address in this letter because they cause the most difficulty in one's life. But since everyone has the ability to change them, all is not lost. Know this, Dear One: you no longer have to be attached to something that is not true about you. You can free yourself and let go of any thought or belief that does not serve you well. One of the greatest mottos in your world is, "Know thyself." When you know yourself on a deeper level, you will know the nature of others. When you have compassion for your own inner child, you will not judge the little one in others. When you are able to forgive how you have treated yourself, you will be able to forgive those who trespass against you. If more people delve into the deep waters of their unknown selves, your world will change. This will happen one day, for your world has entered a new age of Brotherhood. Many more lifetimes will pass before your world changes its own core belief in separateness to a belief in Oneness. But it will happen. If you can find the courage to see what is under the ocean, it is exactly this kind of adventure that will save you, save others, and eventually save your world.

By taking the step of knowing yourself as deeply as you can right now, you will have taken the most important step ever for any lifetime. Knowing the self will always give you the opportunity to know your soul, Dear One, and this knowing is the answer to everything.

Feelings Are Not Truths

Dear One,

It is the investigation of your feelings that has led you to where you are today. I am not saying that your feelings are the sole reason for your growth. Rather, they have been the catalysts that propelled you into the deeper recesses of your being. This is why God gave us feelings: to help the human self begin its journey inward to discover what needs to be overcome and what needs to be celebrated.

Writing you a letter about feelings is not an easy task because it is not a subject easily simplified. The human personality is complex. So I will start with one of the most important tenets about feelings, which is that if you want to know yourself, you must allow yourself to have all of them. This may sound simple enough, but it is not. To allow yourself to have all of your feelings means that you must accept the ones you call "negative" as unconditionally as the ones you call "positive." You cannot possibly be the person you want to be without permitting yourself to honor both. I say this because many spiritual seekers have the misconception that in order to be spiritual, they must concentrate only on positive feelings. Although it is important to think in a positive manner, it is also important to remember that, while in this human lifetime, you must have all the feelings that go with being human; to dismiss some feelings as having less value than others is a mistake. All feelings need to be allowed, for when they are not, they have the power to hold you hostage and upset both the emotional and physical areas of your life.

When you understand that there are no good, bad, right, or wrong feelings, you are headed in the right direction. Duality resides in everything on the Earth plane, including your feelings. Every feeling has a negative and positive aspect, but the feeling itself is not good or bad. Just as one end of a battery is positive and the other is negative, this does not make one end good and the other bad.

It is important to remember, Dear One, that you do not have to like what you feel, but it will help if you can *allow* what you feel without judgment. If you do not label your feelings as good or bad, then you will be more able to give yourself permission to have them. And once you do this, you will lessen the fear of examining them because judgment will no longer have any control over you.

I use the example of guilt frequently because it is one of the most reoccurring feelings in which humans tend to wallow. If you feel guilty about something and label this feeling as "bad," the next step, many times without your awareness, is to associate yourself as *being* "bad." If this occurs, the natural impulse is to want to get rid of the guilt as soon as possible so you no longer think you're bad. Everyone has their own way of doing it. Most often, however, human beings find a way to deal with their guilty feelings by accepting a form of inner punishment that will atone for their perceived wrongdoing. More often than not, this will take the form of finding a way to diminish their happiness. In this way, they feel they have paid for their crime.

I tell you this because this unconscious kind of thinking is a common pattern in your world. So when you do not allow yourself to accept that it is permissible to have a feeling of guilt without judging yourself, you are stuck between a rock and a hard place when it comes to creating more happiness in your life. One part of you believes that you deserve to have what you want and, based on the guilt you are paying for, the other believes that you do not deserve this. This is how human beings sabotage their greatest desires. If you do not allow yourself to have negative feelings without judging them, those feelings will take on tremendous energy with which to create negative outcomes.

Since all creation is based on thought, it is important to remember that feelings are also derived from thought. If you pay attention to a feeling and then rewind in your head what you were just thinking, you will see the definite correlation between the thought and the feeling. A feeling cannot come about on its own. It is always provoked by a preceding thought. For example, a feeling of jealousy occurs because the underlying thought is "I am insecure." A feeling of anxiety comes about because its underlying thought is "I do not trust I can cope." A feeling of anger surfaces because the thought is "I am not able to make everything go my way." Therefore, in order to understand what it is you feel, you must be willing to pay attention to the underlying thoughts that are creating these feelings and then change the thoughts. When you do this, your feelings can change in a split second.

Throughout My letters to you, Dear One, I will be talking frequently about feelings, because they are your greatest teachers. However, you are not your feelings, nor do they tell the truth about you. You are not a failure because you feel like one. You are not defective because you are imperfect. You are not a loser because you made a mistake. You are not weak because you feel vulnerable. And you are not a fool because you feel foolish. Your feelings will never indicate who you are as a person. They only indicate what you are thinking about yourself at any given moment.

There is one exception, however, to this statement that feelings are not truths, and I have saved this for last. The *one* truth that your feelings *will* always tell you is whether or not you are connected or disconnected from Me, your Source of love, happiness, peace, and well-being. When you are feeling love or any derivative of it, such as joy, kindness, or compassion, you are in total alignment with Me.

You are feeling and experiencing the soul of you. Whether you are feeling this for yourself, another person, a pet, your flowers, or a beautiful day, know that in that moment you are totally plugged in to your Godness. You have asked me many times to make Myself known to you. I am telling you now that your true essence is love, and nothing else. Therefore, whenever you have the feeling of expansion within you, that swelling of love in your heart in any way, you are perfectly in line with who you really are.

Your negative feelings, however, are also valuable. They come to teach you that you have jumped track from your Divine self to your ego self – from the soul of you to the humanness of you. Once again, I remind you that this is not a bad thing. You're supposed to be human. It just means you now have the choice to choose whether you are going to get back on track with your Source of well-being or not. Your feelings are a barometer in your life. They show you quite clearly whether or not you are experiencing your human self or your soul self. There is no greater gift your feelings can give you than that, because once you know this, you have the opportunity to make another choice and realign with Me, which always feels so much better. How to do that is another story, which is what the rest of the book is all about.

Therefore, Dear One, no matter what you are feeling, accept what it is you feel and celebrate the fact that you have the power to change it. Rejoice in your ability to know the difference between what you feel as a soul and what you feel as a human. It will help bring balance into your life. Don't be afraid to embrace your humanness. You're not expected to be perfect, so release the fear of experiencing all of your feelings, for when you are less afraid of them, you will be less afraid of you. And when you are less afraid of you, you won't be afraid of knowing Me. After all, you did not come back to this Earth to be less human, Dear One. You came here to experience being *more* human, with your soul leading the way. It is your feelings that are going to help you find the breadcrumbs out of the forest so you can find your way Home. For when you accept and embrace all the feelings of who you are as a human being, you are on the path of knowing yourself as Divine.

It is in the Mundane That the Brownie Points Are Won

Dear One,

Life on Earth is everything I thought it would be, not only because I have been here many times, but also because I know its essence. I arrived here with the full knowledge, expectation, and excitement that life was going to be filled with wonders, adventures, roller coaster rides, opportunities, contrast, beauty, reunions, and challenges. This is the way of Earthly life. Knowing all this, I entered, filled with the desire to experience it all.

Every human being houses his or her own soul, which comes to this Earth plane to experience its own Light. Therefore, everyone is spiritual, whether they acknowledge it or not. Your spirituality can never be apart from you. It functions with your every thought and action. You bring it into every phase of your life and to every encounter and exchange with another, no matter the relationship. I tell you this, Dear One, because often the last place "spirituality" is sought after is in the small, ordinary details of life. And yet, this is exactly where it resides.

Your everyday life is the material you have to work with for experiencing your spirituality. It is where all the tiny miracles take place. So if you keep on waiting for something "big" to happen because you are "spiritual," you are missing the boat. It is the mundane, the everyday practice of living, that gives you the opportunity to remember who you are so you can fulfill the purpose you instigated before you arrived. You and I are here together to experience the everyday phenomena of life.

I must remind you that your growth as a human and your evolvement as a soul do not depend on whether or not you find a cure for cancer, solve the problems of world hunger, advocate for world peace, or give up your possessions. You do not have to perform spectacular works in order to live a spectacular life. Your soul growth, or "brownie points," as I call them, will be determined by how you think, feel, and act toward yourself and others every day of your life.

It is easy to write off the small incidents of life as having little meaning, and yet they are actually important ingredients for growth. For example, did you know that when your grandmother used to knead dough for bread, without realizing it she was not only meditating, but also working out her so-called "problems" of life? Back then, before therapy was in vogue, it was her therapy. It may have appeared to be a menial task, but it had great value for her and helped her to grow. When looking back on your life as a child, do you remember the particular day when a woman came up to you and told you what nice teeth you had? It was a life-changing moment for you. One sentence from this complete stranger transformed your life, because the little girl you once were felt that she had some value and, because of that, she began to smile more often. That one small exchange gave you the confidence you needed to start believing in yourself. Instances like these, Dear One, are the subtle miracles of life which can appear so minute that they get overlooked. And this is why many people fail to see how the Divine takes place in the smallest arenas of life.

The other day, one of those tiny miracles happened within you, even though you never thought of it this way. While in your bathroom you spied a small spider in the corner. Instead of stepping on it (because I know you are not at all fond of these creatures) you actually told the spider that if it didn't come into your bedroom and bite you, you would let it live. You did this because at that exact moment you had the thought that God is in everything, including this eight-legged being. You were actually listening to Me. You then took that thought to the next level, concluding that your husband or dog might kill it. So you got a glass, placed it over the spider, inserted a wash-cloth underneath the glass, squeamishly carried it outside, let the spider go, and wished it well.

That, Dear One, was a brownie point for you. It was not because you didn't kill the spider, because the spider would have continued to live anyway, since even spiders have souls. It was because you remembered that the essence of God also lived within that little being and you wanted it to live as long as it could. You showed respect for a life other than your own. In that way you did something quite mundane and small in the grand scheme of things that was at the same time *huge* in terms of remembrance. And that is what everyday life is all about: remembering what it is you already know and acting on it.

There is not a day that goes by that does not give you the opportunity to grow as a human and evolve as a soul. Listen to what you are thinking and feeling. Notice how you are reacting. When a car cuts you off in traffic or races by you on the highway, do you hope a policeman will pull the driver over, or do you wish the driver a safer journey? Which choice do you make, spite or concern? When you spill something on the floor, do you call yourself "stupid," or do you laugh at yourself? Which choice do you make, to love or to criticize? When you see someone having a hard time loading groceries into a car, do you pass by or do you volunteer to help? Which do you choose, to serve or to ignore? When you notice a mother scolding her child, what goes through your mind? Do you judge her for being a bad mother or do you feel compassion because she may be having a bad day or may not have had a loving mother herself? When life seems to consume you with its hectic pace, do you forget the blessings that surround you, or do you take a moment to say hello to the little yellow butterfly that just drifted past your window? Moment by moment, Dear One, it is the simple things in life that give you the good fortune to live the spiritual life you wish for.

If you can get up every day with the thought that today is the most important day of your life, it will remind you to stay present in each moment, which is where all Creation takes place. It will help you see daily life as the true miracle it is. And this thought will guide you to remembering that you are not just a physical being living a human life. You are also Me, the Divine Observer, who loves you through all the situations of your life, no matter what you create. Every day you spend on this Earth is an honor and a privilege, and you have earned the right to be here. Always remember, Dear One, that the brownie points of life are not won through the big things. They are gained in the wondrous little moments that give you the opportunity to truly experience what life is all about: the joy of living, loving, and evolving.

Section III:

Open These Letters When You Want to Feel in Control of Your Life

You Always Have a Choice

Dear One,

There is nothing more exciting for a soul beginning its Earthly journey than the thought of creating life through the vehicle of choice. It is choice that determines how quickly or slowly a soul in human form evolves. This is not just about choices such as whom to marry, what career to pursue, whether or not to have children, or which vacation will give you the most pleasure. While such choices will certainly affect your life and growth, the choices I refer to are made on an everyday basis. These choices include what you are thinking and feeling, and how you are acting. These, Dear One, are the most powerful choices you will ever make in life.

Not a day goes by without a choice as to how you are going to live that day. You are like a gifted artist with an indescribable palette of colors at your disposal. You can paint your mood for the day with the same colors as yesterday, or you can choose a new variety of colors to paint a different mood. From the moment you wake up, you have a blank canvas to work from. If your day feels emotionally drab and gray, it is because you are painting it that way through what you are thinking. In reality, there is no such thing as a boring day. If you see your day as boring, it's because you have made the choice not to see it as the awesome adventure it is.

In My earlier letter that said it is in the mundane that the brownie points of life are won, I emphasized the importance of seizing the day and paying attention to the little miracles that occur in each moment. Not only do they exist because life itself is a miracle, but also because you can choose to create them. Choice is the essence of creation. From moment to moment, Dear One, you can continually choose new ways of thinking and feeling. Even a negative thought is a choice. When you pay closer attention to the kinds of choices you are making, you can see how you might have painted your day in the darkest colors. If you are having what you would call a "bad day," it is only because things are not going the way you want them to. However, when you give yourself permission to accept what you cannot control and adopt a positive mindset to lead you through the rest of the day, your "bad day" will disappear. For it is you, and you alone, who controls how you are going to feel.

To illustrate the importance of choice, here is an example from a day in your life some years ago. You were standing in the stationary aisle of a store, looking at Mother's Day cards. I know talking about this memory makes you feel a little uncomfortable because you no longer harbor the feelings I will speak of. However, this is exactly why talking about this scenario is so important. This particular day was influential in allowing yourself to feel more positive by investigating what it was you were feeling as you stood there in the store. Using this example can also help the reader to see how choices made in the mind contribute not only to one's sense of well-being, but also to one's evolution as a soul. Although this particular story may seem trivial, it is not. It is rich with significance and powerful beyond measure. Thank you, Dear One, for allowing Me to tell it.

Mother's Day was the following week. Standing in front of the card section, you breathed a heavy sigh, wondering which card to choose. The mushy ones didn't fit at all. You began to feel irritated. Just looking at all the "Mom, you were always there for me" cards triggered your resentment and sadness over not having had the kind of mother you wanted. When those feelings came upon you, you were faced with a myriad of choices, and the real choice that day was not going to be which card to select. It was going to be about which choice would be your teacher and also set your mood for the rest of the day.

Here are the choices that lay before you:

Choice #1: You could stand there and remain filled with sadness and resentment. This, of course, would be a choice that would continue your negative feelings, and your suffering throughout the day.

Choice #2: You could choose the path of acceptance. Knowing that you are a result of your own history and how you were raised, you could choose to see that your mother is also the result of hers. When you think of your own issues and how you have made mistakes because of them, you could decide to give your mother the same understanding. By choosing acceptance, you could choose to diminish your suffering.

Choice #3: Instead of focusing on what your mother didn't give you, you could choose to focus on what she did give you. In other words, you could look for what was right, rather than what was wrong. You may not have received the affectionate mothering you were looking for, but what things *did* she give you that were valuable?

Choice #4: You could say to yourself in anticipation, "Mother's Day is coming up and I have a tendency to feel a little melancholy around this time because the little girl in me can still be triggered by all those overly sweet cards. Perhaps I can be a better mother to her and give her more attention."

Choice #5: You could look at the big picture from a spiritual perspective. It would sound like this: "I came into this life, and as a soul, I chose to be with my mother so we could erase our karma. What an accomplishment this has been! Instead of my bemoaning the fact that I didn't get what I wanted, which was part of the plan, I need to remember that this plan was set forth by Me in the first place for My own growth. Without having had this experience, I might not have had the tendency to look within as much as I have. I can see that the end result has been worth it, because look where I am now. Therefore, I bless my mother for her part in my growth, and I wish her well.

Choice #6: That was then. This is now. The past is over. There is only the present moment in which to say, "What feeling would I prefer to have right now instead of resentment? How can I make that happen? What thoughts do I need to have to reverse this feeling, or at the very least, diminish it?" (By the way, any of the above choices, other than choice #1, would have done the trick.)

Choice #7: *The choice you made.* After thinking through a few of the above thoughts, you bought a beautiful blank card, wrote on it your thanks to your mother for the $1.50 a week she sacrificed to give you piano lessons, which led to your joy of creating music. You also told her how grateful you were for the long hours she worked and for being the strong person she had to be.

Years before, Dear One, you would have bought any card, signed it, put a stamp of obligation on it, and sent it on its merry way. But this time you chose differently as you stood there in the aisle. It only took a few minutes of thought, and you left the store with a feeling of compassion and lightness, and walked out coloring your day sunny yellow.

Every day of your life gives you the opportunity to choose how you will think, feel, and act. Each moment holds a new choice for you if you want it. Free will functions in every moment of your life, whether you realize it or not. Whether you use your free will to your advantage is up to you. Many in your world would rather believe that they do not have a choice, thereby avoiding responsibility for what happens in their life. But there will never be a time in your existence when you do not have a choice. Therefore, the more aware you become of the mental and emotional choices you make, the less likely you are to choose suffering. And this, Dear One, will lead you onto the path of feeling more in control of your life. When you are no longer the pawn of your own feelings, and you realize that you have the power to change them, you will become empowered.

Now I shall remind you of the "magic words" given by your spiritual mentor to help you dismantle negative feelings so you can make more positive choices. With the exception of a major crisis or loss, these two powerful words will give you permission to let go of the importance you are placing on the everyday nuisances of life. These magic words are "So what." "The weather is awful. So what? I have to lose time out of my day to run these errands. So what? I get the feeling this person doesn't like me. So what? I can't believe it's time to pay the taxes again. So what? This grocery line is too long? So what?" "So-whatting" your way through the trivia of life will free you from the negative ego that needs to continue the drama of what is wrong with life and what it thinks is wrong with you. These magic words can lift your spirit and get you to a place where you can say, "I can still be happy, even if life isn't happening the way I want it to." Therefore, give yourself permission to say, "So what?" to the things in life that don't really matter. Now, that, Dear One, is a great choice and one that will lead you to freedom.

When I made the decision to come into physical form once more, I came anticipating the excitement of making new choices for My next creation through a new time period to learn from, a new agenda to follow for My soul growth, and a new body. The greatest choice I have ever made is having you as My human personality. The choices you make as a human being will affect how we both grow and evolve. This may sound like quite a responsibility, and it is. It is a responsibility every human being has to his or her soul. But know this, Dear One, it is also the greatest honor you will ever have. Fall in love with the idea of choice, embrace it as the empowering gift it

79

is, and use it consciously to create the life you have always wanted. In essence, this is what life is all about.

Responsibility is Your Key to Freedom

Dear One,

There is a point in everyone's life when he or she comes to a fork in the road and must choose which path to take. This is not a road encountered every year or so. It is a road you are faced with every day of your life. It is the road of responsibility, the road less taken.

Everything I have written to you thus far has led us to this road. It is not for the faint of heart. It takes tremendous courage to walk this road, for it is not easy to acknowledge that you are responsible for what you think, feel, and do, which, fundamentally, leads to the creation of your life. Clearly, to take responsibility for these things is not the easy way out, which is why many do not choose this path. Instead, they choose the path of blame.

In your world, the word, "responsibility," most often assumes a negative connotation. It can suggest a burden of some sort, such as, "I am tired of having all this responsibility." Other times it can imply blame, as in "It's not my fault. I'm not the one responsible." These are negative examples of responsibility. The kind of responsibility I am talking about, however, is based on joy and freedom which sounds like this, "No one else in my life is responsible for what I am thinking. No one else in my life is responsible for what I feel. No one else can possibly claim ownership of how I act. Everything I think, feel, and do creates a vibration which propels itself into the Universe and comes back to me in whatever form it was sent out. If I focus on taking responsibility for what happens in my life, I will recognize that I am the ultimate authority of my life, and the only one who has the power to change it. I will then awaken to the fact that I, and I alone, hold the key to the self-imposed prison to which I am confined, and I will no longer need to believe that I am a victim of life. Instead, I will be able to see myself as a powerful Creator. If I can truly see the connection between the energy that goes out of me and that which comes back to me, I will have full awareness of my ability to create. If I can take responsibility and own my Divinity as the Creator of my life, it will mean that I can now accept being more powerful than I ever imagined. And with that acceptance comes a freedom, sometimes seemingly scary, that will become the greatest delight of my life."

This, Dear One, is where the road ends for most people, for there is a great resistance to being that powerful and having that kind of freedom. The kind of power that comes with such responsibility frightens many, because it implies the ultimate surrendering of one's victimhood and giving up blame. When you remain the victim, you expect others to take care of you in some way. Thinking you are owed something, you then retain your helplessness and refuse to recognize your part in the play of life. On a global level, all one has to do is watch the nightly news to see the blaming and fear of taking responsibility in action.

While you cannot be responsible for everything that happens in your world, you can be accountable for what happens in your life. This means recognizing that every choice you make – whether through thought, word, or deed – has a consequence that will affect you. Taking responsibility can be anything from owning your feelings, to taking a closer look at what continues to show up in your life. When given consideration and worked on, taking responsibility is one of the major pillars in a human life that can help a soul evolve more quickly through its journey.

The quickest and most effective way to begin this undertaking is to start with owning what it is you feel. If you were to do just that and nothing else, your life would change immensely for the better. However, this notion is not popular because Society teaches you to say, "You make me feel (*fill in the blank*)." In fact, "you make me" is one of the most debilitating statements in life. By making someone else responsible for what comes out of your heart, you not only make someone else more powerful than you, you also hand over the responsibility to them for making you feel better. If you do that, your next step would be to get that other person to react differently so you can feel okay. Now you have just given control over your life to someone else because you can't feel better unless they change. Oh my!

Taking responsibility, Dear One, goes hand in hand with choice. For example, if someone says something and you feel angry because of it, the first thing to do is acknowledge to yourself that you are feeling angry. The next hurdle is: can you own that feeling without blaming the other person? It is true that he or she was certainly a catalyst and triggered your angry feeling, but no one forced you to have that feeling. You could have chosen from a number of feelings in response to that person's remark, but you chose to feel angry. Since your response may have been automatic, it may not seem as though you made a choice. But the truth is that no one but you, Dear One, decided which feeling to pull out of your emotional hat.

Your next venture will be to look within and examine why you felt irritated. Was it because there was some truth that you didn't want to hear in the other person's statement? Was it because you expected a different response from that person? Was it because you took what was said personally? If you say "yes" to any of these questions, you are on the path of taking responsibility. You are becoming a being who feels deeply, acknowledges those feelings, and takes responsibility for either keeping them or changing them. When you practice taking responsibility for what you feel without blaming someone else, you will have accomplished one of the greatest successes of human life. You are now empowering yourself to change within, without expecting another to change for you. Even if you choose to keep feeling angry, how long you stay in it is still your responsibility. Taking responsibility is a process that will continue throughout your life and will bring you the immense rewards of becoming a healthier, more loving, more powerful human being. And this will free you from thinking that someone else is in charge of your life. In essence, you will put yourself in control of how you react. You will be in the driver's seat of your existence, which will change your life in more ways than you can imagine because freedom will be right there at your doorstep.

There is one example about the importance of taking responsibility for your life that I want to mention in this letter, Dear One. This was when you broke your foot. For weeks prior to falling in the pot-hole, your daily thought was, "I need a break. I *really* need a break." You knew that you needed to take time off from work because you were tired, but you would not allow yourself to do so. Needing a rest dominated your thoughts. Your feelings were also trying to tell you that time off was needed. You felt tired and irritable. Everything in your being conveyed a longing for rest. So, the Universe responded to your "request" by giving you back exactly what you vibrationally sent forth. Not only did you get that literal "break" in your foot, but you were also forced to take time off from work and get the "break" you so desperately needed. It was not the vacation you had in mind, but you got what you asked for. To those who do not believe in the power of creation through thought vibration, this example may sound ludicrous. But I tell you, it is not. This is how powerful you are to create what happens in your life without your awareness. Everyone is this powerful.

I have used this small example because it illustrates the importance of believing in yourself as a Creator and taking responsibility for what you create, even when you may not be pleased with the outcome. This incident illustrates how you created something which initially appeared negative, but then brought you absolute joy when you realized that your broken foot was not an "accident." When you made the connection between your thoughts and feelings of needing a rest and the actual manifestation of a broken foot resulting in a break from work, a light bulb went off in your head. You discovered the common denominator. You witnessed the power of your creation. It finally made you a true believer.

The growth connected to this, Dear One, was that you did not beat yourself up for creating it. Instead, you chuckled and thought, "If I can create something like this, what else could I possibly create that could be even more desirable?" And the experience of this little episode of the broken foot led you to a far greater place of awareness than you had ever known. It was an awakening, because the idea of you being the Creator of your life was no longer simply intellectual. Everyone has the ability to have this kind of awakening when they take a closer look at the correlation between what goes on in their mind and what shows up in their life.

When you take charge of your life by taking responsibility for it, you are living the life of the spiritual warrior. No matter what it is you create, whether it appears negative or positive, the outcome is always there to serve and teach you what you need to know at any given point in your life. If you can release judgment from the outcome, the word "responsibility" takes on a whole new meaning.

When you begin to work on taking responsibility for your feelings and for seeing how your thoughts affect your reality, you are on the road less traveled. This road will give you a newfound freedom that says, "I do not have to be a victim of myself, of another, or of life anymore. If I create something unwanted, I can change it to something else." This is true power, Dear One. This is the kind of freedom everyone wants, but few seek or work to earn. If more people would take this huge step and give themselves the gift of taking responsibility, the rest of the world would follow suit.

What I want you to remember, Dear One, is that responsibility is not an onus or a burden. It is a privilege. Responsibility is the key to owning your birthright as a soul. By accepting that you have responsibility for how your life turns out, you are using the greatest gift of the Creator, the ability to awaken to the awareness that you are an eternal being with the power, strength, and genius to create your own happiness and make your life what you want it to be. The more you take responsibility, the freer you will be. And the freer you are, the more joyous your life will be.

The Journey Will Always Trump the Arrival

Dear One,

There are many people in your world who want tomorrow today. They want what they want, and they want it now. Impatience is an everyday reaction because there are so many things you can obtain instantly and so few you have to wait for. Just look at the restlessness people exhibit when waiting in line, and you will see what I mean. Years ago, people had to wait for the bread to rise, the mail to arrive by train, the vegetables to grow, and the clothes to dry. Patience was a necessity. There were no supermarkets to provide food – no email, no online shopping, no phoning or texting from anywhere in the world.

Today, the need for instant gratification has lessened the value of patience, and has created a Society that becomes frustrated when things do not happen in the anticipated time frame. Consequently, there is an underlying longing for a magic pill to cure physical and emotional problems, troubled relationships, and general unhappiness. Although epidemic impatience may be the price we pay for technological progress, it also can be a lesson in learning the beauty of patience. This is exactly why living in your world today offers you an unlimited opportunity for soul growth. Patience, Dear One, always leads to soul growth. And patience is the ingredient needed for your evolution in the most important and eternal aspect of your life, which is process.

You cannot blossom into the being you want to be without going through the necessary unfolding. A flower is not intent on escalating its growth process. First it is a seed which is tended with sunlight and moisture. Then, in its right and perfect time it will sprout and grow. This is also how life works for you. The purpose of the experience of being human is to enable you to move through the process of life. It gives you the time you need to go through many different stages of maturation and growth on both the physical and spiritual levels. Each human being has a unique process unlike that of any other.

What makes life such an adventure is its movement. Process is like the rhythm of God's breath, which you like to call the wave in the ocean. You move forward and back, just as you breathe in and out. The process of life is in continual motion. Even when you feel stuck in life, you are still moving, whether you know it or not. In order to move forward in any area of your life, you have to be willing to go through what it takes to get to the other side. You will never be able to microwave your process, even though you may try, because the only way out is through.

For example, you thought this book should have been written and published by the time you were forty. When it was not, you thought something was wrong with your writing. When you arrived at age fifty and the book was still not written, you were disappointed in yourself, thinking you just weren't motivated or disciplined enough to get the job done. Yet, by the time you reached sixty and the book was still not published, your attitude had changed. You stopped worrying about when it would be finished and instead began to lighten up, because by then you had come to believe that everything comes to fruition in its right and perfect time. As you let go of the worry and believed in the process, you discovered that the book began to flow. You needed those extra twenty years, Dear One, to reach the maturity and trust essential to believing in yourself, believing in this book, and believing in the power of process. Given the nature of the book's content, those twenty extra years were also needed for the world to be ready to hear your message. So, you see, nothing went wrong. Nothing was out of place. Nothing should have been different. It was all part of your process.

One of the most important functions of patience throughout the process of life is to remind you that the journey is much more rewarding than the arrival. If you were to ask someone which journey was more enjoyable and exciting, taking a road trip from the east coast to the west coast or flying from New York to Los Angeles in five hours, there would be no contest. This is true of the journey of life. What makes you take longer to move toward your destination may make for a much more rewarding venture. Doubtless, holding this book in your hand one day will be a wonderful feeling, but the journey of the process of writing it is what will truly touch your heart. And in life, Dear One, it is the passage that is important, not the destination. Your life is an extraordinary ride that will continue on to the next adventure and the next. Therefore, there will never be an end to your process because there is no end to you. Ever.

Every road you will follow in this lifetime must be traveled in its own right and perfect time. As your soul, I have been given everything I need to accomplish what I set out to do during My years with you on this Earthly plane. Growth is a process. What I need from you is the patience to wait for the right and perfect unfolding that will enable it to happen. Nothing happens before its time – not the flower, not the wine, not your life. The more you know this in your heart, the less you will suffer when things don't go the way you think they should. Whenever you feel the frustration of impatience, just whisper to yourself "soul growth." It will put a smile on your face and ease your heart.

Dear One, I am the part of you that can see the bigger picture much more clearly than you can. Trust in Me. Plant your seeds of desire. Know what you want and send those thoughts lovingly on their way into the Divine Universe. Then patiently and faithfully wait for what you want to come to you. Meanwhile, accept and lovingly acknowledge that no matter what goal you have set for yourself, the process of the journey is always the most satisfying part of getting there.

It's Not What Happens to You in Life, It's How You Handle It

Dear One,

As you know, life is said to work in mysterious ways, and it is true that in one lifetime you cannot possibly know all the answers to its mystery. But when you understand how life works and how you can feel more in control of it, your existence is not as mysterious as you may think. I have written in depth about thought being the foundation for all creation. From there, thought creates feelings which give you the gift of knowing whether or not you are in alignment with your soulful self or your human self. The third component of creation comes about as a direct result of what you are thinking and feeling, which is how you are going to react in any given situation. These components are the "chain of command" that leads you to become aware of how you create your life.

There are many ways reactions are exhibited. If you are thinking and feeling negatively, for example, the usual reaction will also manifest some form of negativity. If you are feeling annoyed with someone, you might react by expressing direct anger toward them. Or you could say nothing and let it fester inside of you, allowing anger turned inward to make you feel depressed. You could find yourself driving too fast, obsessing over the situation to the extent that you are mindlessly endangering yourself and others. You might start a pointless, irrelevant argument with your spouse or have an absolutely miserable time at a planned outing with friends. You could overeat, oversleep, and overindulge in just about anything.

These are just a few negative reactions one can have. Some are direct, some are not. Since confrontation is an aspect of growth feared by Society, most people will select the less direct route.

I tell you this, Dear One, because looking closely at your reactions is essential to feeling you have more control over your life. There will always be situations and incidents in your life that you cannot control. Most important, what you *can* control is your reaction to them. Reaction takes creation to a whole new level because, as an extremely active experience, it easily attracts similar reactions. Negativity begets negativity. When you react strongly to something, it gathers momentum like a giant tumbleweed. It is wonderful when the reaction is positive, but it can be harmful when it is not.

Many people react automatically and consequently do not take responsibility for the thoughts that created the reaction in the first place. Since you are responsible for how you think, feel, and react, no one can make you react in a certain way, and no incident is powerful enough to keep you angry for the rest of your life without your own permission.

There is no doubt that you have come here this time around to be presented with various life situations that will encourage you to challenge yourself to experience your soul growth. Therefore, you are not expected to be perfect or to react to everything perfectly. Human life is not easy, nor is it meant to be perfectly happy all the time. But it is also not meant to be a burden. The more you learn how to cope with life, the better life gets. And you learn these coping skills by paying attention to your reactions.

Every experience in your life makes you stronger, wiser, and more able to cope. Every situation leaves a lesson waiting to be discovered and learned. Each experience or situation ultimately leads you to grow and unfold. The more you can purposely choose your thoughts, feelings, and reactions, the more you will begin to experience the fullness of life and see that God is alive "in living color" within you. Out of everything comes soul growth, Dear One. Although in your human mind you may not think that this is enough or even worth it, in your spiritual reality it is everything!

One of the best ways of understanding and controlling your reactions is to ask yourself the very important question, "What am I learning about myself in this situation?" This question alone will not only lead you to a different perception of what is going on, but will also help you cope with *anything*. It has the potential to slow down your obsession with the given circumstance, take the onus off the situation, and place the focus on you. It can also give you the impetus to keep your head up during trying times, knowing that this experience will help you gain something. Perceiving what you are learning from a situation, rather than focusing on the situation itself, can actually make the event more tolerable.

Look at the happenings in your life as learning experiences. Do you remember when your fear of not passing your social work licensing exam created such anxiety within that you were on pins and needles for days? Through that experience you learned how much you really wanted to continue to work so you could be of service to others. When you had an overnight hospital stay you learned that being irritated over unloading the dishwasher is nothing. When you reacted to a negative comment from a friend, you learned that you do not have the right words for everyone and every situation. When you broke your foot, you learned how much your patients cared and remained loyal to you. And when your mother passed, you remembered how much you have always loved her, and how much she really did love you.

Focusing on your reactions to any life situation rather than on the situation itself will not only lessen the impact it has over you, but will also help you learn to cope with it. Keep asking yourself, "What am I learning from this?" Sometimes the answers can be as simple as "patience," "receiving from others," "I am not alone," or "people care about me more than I thought." Do not see these answers as miniscule. For they *could* be the very same areas of soul growth you asked for long before you got here. And whether you see it as positive or negative, each situation provides the impetus for you to discover yourself.

When you begin to look at life from a Higher perspective, through My eyes, you will begin to react differently. If you can bear in mind that you are gaining soul growth by remembering that you are learning from everything that comes to you, you will begin to change your attitude toward whatever comes your way. You will actually discover that you have the ability to feel peaceful, even during a difficult time. And when that happens, you will begin to attract more experiences that bring peace and wellbeing. This is how you can learn to heal yourself in any situation. It is a spiritual process, if you choose to see it that way. If you can look for the Higher mindset, you will always find Me in you. The more you are able to react from this place while being human, the more you will evolve into who you really are. And that is the point of being here, Dear One, to remember and experience your Divinity while feeling your humanity to its fullest.

94

Dancing with Ego

Dear One,

I knew when I made the decision to come back into a physical lifetime that the dance between soul and human would take place. Being plummeted into the world of the human psyche always requires the dance with ego. It is a dance all souls are excited about, look forward to, and are ready and eager to participate in. However, it is a very complicated dance, with intricate steps, and one that requires many dance lessons before it can be mastered.

My desire in writing this letter is to help you see ego in a different light, so you can understand it and know how to manage it in your life. Many teachings, both spiritual and secular, encourage the renunciation of ego in order to reach enlightenment or perfection. Do not feel defective if you cannot do this, because it is actually impossible. One can diminish, or even overcome, the power the ego has in a lifetime, but one cannot rid one's self of it.

The Creator does not make mistakes. Ego was created as part of the conscious mind to fulfill a need. It was originally meant to be a reasoning tool that would help Mankind endure. More like a verb than a noun, its job was to provide the "push" to improve and to propel us toward what we desire. In an often dangerous environment, accomplishment was crucial to the survival of early Man. One who could fashion a better spear was more likely to succeed at providing food and staving off predators. At some point, accomplishment took on competitive energy and then brought the desire for power over others. Once survival was intact, humans were free to go in search of their true inner nature, which is Spirit. Ego was meant to be relegated to a small role in the development of the physical life so that the soul could lead. It was meant to be a servant of Humanity, but instead, throughout the Ages became its ruler.

Knowing this, you must understand that ego is not bad. Duality rules everything in your world, and ego is no exception. It has both a positive and negative side. Your positive ego is meant to help you take care of your needs as you go through life. It helps you make decisions, builds your strengths, and supports your identity as an individual among many. It reminds you to take care of yourself and follow your own path. Without your positive ego, you would not be able to adhere to the lessons contained in these letters.

On the other hand, negative ego creates difficulties because its essence is fear. All negative emotions – resentment, hatred, jealousy, greed, guilt, defensiveness, blame, separateness, anger, and more – are born out of fear. In fact, any emotion that makes you feel either badly about yourself or superior to another is evidence that your negative ego is leading the dance. To make your life what you want it to be, you will need to call upon all the strength and courage you have to challenge your negative ego. It is the greatest challenge every soul and its human counterpart will face in a lifetime and an essential pattern in the dance with ego.

However, you must not make an enemy of ego, Dear One, for in doing so you will begin a battle that will not serve you well. Rather, think of your ego as the Wizard of Oz. At first, he appears as a fearsome orb that threatens dire consequences for those who do not meet his needs. But when exposed, the Wizard is just an ordinary little dweeb of a man behind a curtain working a set of controls that make him seem huge and powerful. This is what negative ego looks like. It is that small part of you that uses scare tactics to make you distrust your inner wisdom. In that way, negative ego hopes you will depend on what it has to offer and believe what it has to say. It will also try to convince you that it should remain the dance instructor of your life. It says, "Let me take the lead. I know what I'm doing." In reality, it does not. It only knows one dance, repeating the same steps over and over, encouraging you to believe that you need no other partner.

There is great value in knowing your ego, because it is one of your greatest teachers. Since it consistently presents you with fear, ego will always give you the opportunity to choose trust. Time and again, it will guide you to choose acceptance by encouraging you to judge. When it promotes resentment, it will challenge you to embrace forgiveness. Because it constantly creates drama, it will give you the opportunity to create peace. You cannot make the positive choices you want in life without first being tested by your negative ego. This, Dear One, is its greatest role: to give you the choice to overcome your own suffering. Negative ego is the catalyst you need in order to grow and evolve. It is here to be the Darth Vader of your existence so you can choose to be the Light. You must have darkness in the physical world in order for you to overcome it. The reality of who you are is Light, and your humanness is the vehicle used to let that Light shine through. This is how you evolve. You are here in this lifetime to diminish that which is negative in you so the dance between us can become an elegant, graceful waltz between human and Spirit.

If you want Me to take the lead in the dance and guide you joyously and peacefully through your life, you must be willing to pull back the curtain and see the fearful and insecure part of you for what it is. You must look hard at your ego and then open yourself to the concept that profound happiness is your birthright. If you want this, you must find the courage and discipline to recognize when your negative ego takes the lead, keeping you stuck in the same old thoughts and feelings, cavorting about in the same old dance, again and again. I will explain this further in the next letter, Dear One, because it is vitally important to your growth. Ultimately, it will be you, the human part of Me, who will decide through free will who will lead the dance of your life.

The Thirty Second Rule

Dear One,

Years ago, when you were told the "Thirty Second Rule" by your spiritual mentor, you were not only astonished at the concept, but also very resistant to the idea. Your ego was kicking and screaming at the idea of the thirty second rule because it felt threatened, and still does, by the idea of anything lessening its control over you. And that is exactly the purpose of this spiritual rule: to decrease the ego's influence so you can choose to let Spirit lead the dance of your life. I understand the hesitation you felt at the time, because challenging yourself to even think about the Thirty Second Rule is not for the faint-hearted. In fact, it is probably one of the most difficult feats any human being can strive to accomplish. Therefore, Dear One, know that performing this rule in thirty seconds is not expected of you. It is something to work toward. The Thirty Second Rule is not actually a "rule." It is a "rule of thumb," or guideline, that can help you recognize when your negative ego gets in the way of your happiness. I will reiterate to you this bit of your spiritual mentor's wisdom because it is an effective tool for empowerment and change. It is as follows:

With the exception of loss, the first thirty seconds of any negative feeling has legitimacy.
After that, it's all ego.

When you first heard these words from your mentor during the session, you had been speaking about an irritating interaction you had with another. When the Thirty Second Rule was explained, your immediate response was to feel annoyed. You thought, "I deserve to have these feelings for more than thirty seconds. I have a lot to be irritated about. It's going to take more than thirty seconds to get over these feelings." At that moment, you were not interested in getting rid of your annoying feeling, nor did you feel ready for a peaceful settlement within. Because you felt justified, you wanted to continue to be angry. And this, Dear One, is what keeps you, or anyone, from being joyous and peaceful. It is the ego's need to feel justified and entitled.

What your spiritual teacher was telling you is that every emotion has a thirty second period of legitimacy, because every feeling comes to tell you something. But when your negative feelings continue past the thirty second mark, it is a sign that your ego is taking the lead in our dance, and it is up to you to choose whether or not you will allow that to continue. The only time this rule does not apply is when one is experiencing a crisis or loss, since bereavement is a process that must progress over time.

Know that the Thirty Second Rule is neither a tool to stifle your feelings, nor a rule that says, "If you cannot do it in that timeframe you are not evolved." Instead, the thirty seconds is something to aspire to and work toward. Rather than something you have to attain in this lifetime, it is a reference to use when a negative thought or feeling haunts you. If the negative feelings continue after hours, days, weeks, or years – ego is leading the way. When you are willing to face your ego and its need for emotional theatrics, however, you will be able to feel more in control of your life.

As you have discovered over the years, there are many feelings you have not wanted to give up because it would mean taking control of your drama. Ego wants to convince you to stay with these negative feelings because it has a need to continue the suffering in your life. It is not that ego is bad. It simply does not know whether it will continue to exist if something bigger and better takes over. In essence, it's afraid of dying. Therefore, in order to abate that fear, it needs to feel entitled with the mindset of being a victim. In that way, it gets your negative attention, thereby making it come "alive."

What I am about to tell you next is the key to identifying and understanding your ego for the rest of your life. And it is this: Ego will always come to the forefront of your life when something is not happening the way you think it should, when someone is not acting or saying something you want to hear, or when expectations you may have are not being met. If you truly think about this when experiencing any negative feeling, you will recognize this as truth. If you are angered by someone's behavior, for example, it is because they are not acting the way you think they should. If you are hurt by what someone says, it is because you are not hearing what you want to hear. When you are disappointed in the world, it is because the world isn't living up to how you want it to be. It is the same when you are disappointed in yourself. It is important to recognize that behind every negative emotion is a desire that is not being met, and when that happens your ego is ready to spring into action. Therefore, it is the humanness of your negative ego that demands that things should be different. You should be different. Others should be different. Life should be different. As you can see, Dear One, the ego has very little tolerance for the concept of acceptance.

Let us go back to your session that day with your mentor. You were feeling irritation about someone because you were not willing to accept who she was. You wanted her to be different. Your desire was for her to be who you wanted her to be, and when she was not, you harbored anger and disappointment. This was *your* ego in full bloom. Not until you began to accept her for who she was did you begin to see the growth that evolved out of this acceptance. Remember that acceptance does not mean that you have to like or condone someone's personality or behavior. It means that you accept that this is who they are, whether you like it or not. When you were able to acknowledge your negative feelings and let them go, ego no longer ruled you in that situation. You felt much better when you let go of the negative burden you were carrying. You see, Dear One, as long as you work on this particular rule of thumb, it does not matter how long it takes. Just the awareness of when your ego is in action is an accomplishment unto itself.

When you allow yourself to be an observer of your feelings, rather than a reactor, a miraculous thing will happen: your negative feelings will begin to subside and lose their full-time residence in your head. Through the process of observation you will be more likely to accept what you feel, without being invested in justifying your feelings. In this frame of mind, you will experience the presence of your true spiritual nature, which cannot succumb to negativity.

By observing your feelings, rather than allowing them to control you, you are in effect holding them as though holding a crying baby. When a baby is held, it calms down. By holding your ego in this way, its effect on you begins to diminish, *not* because it is being soothed, per se, but because it is being *observed*. The ego cannot stand to be seen. It wants to remain hidden. Therefore, once you have discovered the little man behind the curtain and observed him for what he is, he loses his power and hides – until the next time, of course. Meanwhile, you feel better because you are not being ruled by your feelings. Instead, you are in control of them, which adds to feeling more in control of your life.

This is how you diminish ego in your life, Dear One. This is how you take responsibility for the dance between you as a human and Me as your soul, and how you create a better dance for us. The inherent value of the Thirty Second Rule is that it helps you recognize what is happening within you, giving you the opportunity to make another choice.

Like anything, this rule becomes easier when you practice it. This is the simplicity and wisdom of it. It is something you can think about and remember every time you are unhappy. Once you are aware that your ego is up to its usual tricks, it will be up to you to determine what to do with it and how long to stay in it.

The Thirty Second Rule is for those who want to change and make a difference in their life. Once again, it takes courage to apply this concept because there is even more resistance from the ego once it is recognized. The irony is that, when you can approach this wisdom as a game, it becomes easier to live it. It can actually be fun and fairly humorous. It's like saying to your ego, "I see you. I know who you are, little wizard. I see what's going on." This can be very uplifting and empowering once you see the rewards of letting go of self-created suffering. In doing so, you begin to have the most wonderful feeling of love – love for yourself, and love coming from Me. And you will know, without a doubt, that there is nothing you cannot overcome, nothing you cannot have, and nothing you will ever have to fear. You will feel more integrated and balanced. You will be free. Then, Dear One, you will be able to do something you have always wanted to do since you were a child...

You will fly.

Section IV:

Open These Letters When You Want to Diminish Fear and Recapture Happiness

Fear Shows You Where More Love is Needed

Dear One,

As you know, fear is part of the human journey. In its most positive form, fear is a useful teaching tool. It instructs children to respect boundaries so that the hot stove will not burn them and, if they look before crossing the road, the traffic will not be dangerous. Fear can be a motivator for adults, enabling them to become more focused and disciplined. A fearsome diagnosis, for example, can be the instigator to leading a healthier life. If a deadline needs to be met, fear can be the impetus that gets the job done. Fear also triggers the instinct that tells you to run away from something, or releases the adrenaline and summons the strength to withstand it. Therefore, it is important to understand that not all fear is bad. It is a normal emotion that is hard-wired into your DNA for the purpose of survival. It is also useful in warning you to step back and take a second look if something does not feel right. At its very best, fear will always come to tell you something you need to know.

In its negative persona, however, fear is the most debilitating emotion of all, which is why an entire section of this book is devoted to it. As opposed to the feeling of love, which is an expansive one, fear has the opposite effect. It contracts, like one of those little black and brown fuzzy caterpillars that curl into a little ball in your hand when you pick him up. That little guy shrivels in order to protect himself. This is what fear does. It makes you curl up inside yourself and feel small, vulnerable, and helpless. It can creep into your psyche like an insidious fog or can suddenly pull you under like quicksand.

Fear, Dear One, creates separation in your world, not only between individuals, but between countries, as well. The underlying emotion of every judgmental thought, violent act and war, is fear. Your world has a difficult time accepting the differences and uniqueness of its inhabitants. It would rather see everyone be the same, act the same, and believe the same. The result of this mindset is that human beings become fearful of their differences rather than accepting and embracing them. This is why there is nothing more important in your life than understanding how fear plays a part in it, because fear will always keep you in a forgetful space and keep you from moving toward the safety of love. When you allow yourself to confront and diminish your fears, you will lessen fear in the world.

If you were to survey others as to whether or not they think fear plays a large part in their lives, the majority would say that it does not. This is because most people think of fear as something frightening. What many are not aware of, however, is that any number of tributaries branch off of the great river of fear. Worry, anxiety, obsession, and doubt are common extensions of fear. Low self-esteem and vulnerability follow suit. Therefore, when I talk about the importance of reducing fear in your life, Dear One, I am talking about looking at the more subtle aspects and becoming aware of how they influence your everyday life. If people would pay close attention to their feelings for just one hour, they would see how fear is much more prominent in their lives than they might have thought.

Fear manifests itself in the lives of human beings in many ways. Underlying every fear is the belief that one does not have the ability to cope. Think about this for a moment. If you truly believed that you could handle anything that comes your way, do you think you would worry so much? Most likely not. This doesn't mean that you are expected to completely rid yourself of fear, but if you knew you had the inner resources to cope with anything, your fear would lessen tremendously. When you begin to worry about "what if this or that happens?" you are falling into a mindset that says you do not trust that you will be able to handle the circumstances. This is what makes worry, preoccupation and low self-esteem epidemic in your Society. People do not trust in their ability to rise to the occasion and endure.

Whenever you are in the grip of fear, whether large or small, try to remember that you do have the strength to cope with anything, because you have everything you need within yourself to do so. When you allow fear to take up too much space in your heart, it means you have stepped out of alignment with who you really are. You are forgetting that your greatest coping mechanism is your soul, because it is Me that has carried you through every tumultuous experience you have ever had. The more you can accept the premise that you have many more inner resources than you think, the easier it will be to get back on track when fear comes to visit. I encourage you, Dear One, not to run away from any fear that makes its way into your life, no matter how insignificant. Instead, I urge you to run "full steam ahead" toward all of your fears and face them head-on. Avoiding them only keeps your life in a state of continuing drama.

There is no doubt that fear is a doubled-edged sword. On the one hand it can exhaust and weaken you, and on the other hand, it comes to let you know that your belief that you do not have the ability to cope is at the forefront of your mind. Please note that I am not saying that waiting for a loved one's surgery to be over should not produce fearful thoughts as you pace back and forth in the waiting area. Of course it would. Losing your job and not knowing how you will pay the bills would also induce fear. In such situations these are normal fears. The question still is, however: Do you know that you will be able to cope with what happens despite the result? Do you know that you have the strength to handle a situation should you need to?

This is how you handle fear in such circumstances so that it does not overcome you. Within you is a love so profound that, no matter the worry, the Divine in you has the capacity to deal with anything. It is this belief that will help you diminish fear in your life. When you begin to feel afraid, it is important to reach out to the part of you that has *no* fear. And that would be *Me*, the God in you. I will always be your greatest coping mechanism, Dear One, so use Me.

Don't just look up to the heavens and ask God to give you strength. You can do that, but also realize that He has already given you His strength by creating you. Therefore, ask the God within you, as well as the God outside of you, to help you remember the incredible, strong soul you already are. In this way, you are calling upon your own Divine Love to help you heal your fear, for love heals everything.

Here is how you can use Me to your advantage. Sit in a quiet place. Play some comforting music if you like, especially music without words. As you feel a fear stirring within you, call on Me, ask for Me, and visualize Me wrapping My arms around you from the inside out. Picture a golden white Light surrounding every part of you. Breathe deeply and allow yourself to feel what it is you are afraid of or worried about. Now, breathe in the white Light of peace, and breathe out fear. Do this a number of times. As you sit quietly, feel the word "love." Feel the love you have for your spouse or for your animals. Feel the compassion and love you have for yourself or anyone else. You can even call up a memory from the past in which you felt loved. Allow this love to enter your fearsome surroundings during these moments. Now, breathe in the love from that memory. Breathe in the safety. Breathe in your strength. Breathe in the golden white Light that surrounds you. You will find, Dear One, that love and fear cannot occupy the same space at the same time, and as you breathe in love, your fear will begin to diminish.

Know that this love is telling you that you have the ability to cope with whatever you are worried about. It is now time to take a deep breath and remind yourself that throughout your life you have always found a way to endure whatever was in front of you. In fact, there has never been a time when you have not managed to find the strength you were looking for in any situation, even when you were a child.

I am your antidote to fear, Dear One. Since your most natural spiritual talent is the power of thought, hold the powerful thought that fear does not have to rule your life. Take that thought from Me and know with certainty that there is a part of you that fears nothing and that you can call upon that part of you anytime and anywhere.

When fear knocks at your door, let Me be the one to open it, for fear cannot stand to be in My presence. Know that fear in its various disguises no longer has to be the bogeyman it used to be. Instead, let it be a reminder that it is time to reconnect with your loving, Divine nature.

In this way, fear will have served the most Divine purpose it possibly can, because it will have given you the cue to come home to Me. And to be quite honest, Dear One, we cannot ask anything more from fear than that.

Diving to the Depths: The Fear of Yourself

Dear One,

Many human beings in your world are trying to discover who they are because their souls have set forth the intention of remembering their true essence while living an Earthly life. No two souls go about remembering in the same way, which makes the journey of life unique to each and every one. Every soul has an overwhelming desire for its human counterpart to remember that he or she carries the Oneness of God within. And every soul also knows that, to some degree, its human counterpart will resist knowing itself in this way because the fear of self always intercedes. Although this may not seem strange to you, others may be amazed to learn that no greater fear exists.

I am not talking about knowing yourself in terms of your likes and dislikes, or being aware of your various opinions. I am talking about knowing who you are on a deeper level – knowing what makes you tick, what triggers you, and why you think, feel and act a certain way. If I were to use the analogy of water representing your self-awareness, I would say that most people are not afraid of sticking their toes in the water or wading up to their waist. There is no risk or fear in that. It is the depth of the water, Dear One, that frightens the majority of your world, the depth of self and the fear of going under the water. For this is where the deepest self resides. The irony of this is that you are already Infinite Depth. Who you really are is nothing less than deep, and your depth is where the buried treasure lies. Yet, for most, this treasure remains untouched.

As long as you are afraid of knowing yourself more deeply than you already do, it will be difficult to find the treasure within. This fear will not allow you to experience the bigger picture of who you are and how you fit into the world as a human and a soul. You may have an inkling of it. You may read and fantasize about what it means to be both human and Divine. You may even have an intellectual understanding of the bigger picture in terms of God and the Universe. You can read about other people's theories, including Mine, and resonate with them. But until you are willing to take a closer look at yourself and do the inner work of diving to your depths, it will be difficult to *experience* what I am talking about.

As I said in the last letter, fear comes to visit when there is an underlying belief that one is not able to cope with what he or she fears. The reason this belief exists in the first place is because most people do not know themselves deeply enough to fully realize that they do have the ability to cope. Wading up to your waist in the water of awareness will not be enough to know who you really are, because the fear of what might be found under the water keeps most people from going any deeper. This is exactly why the fear of knowing the self needs to be explored "in greater depth."

Therefore, in this letter, it is diving lessons you shall have. If attempted a little bit at a time, they are not as fearsome as one may think. The first thing any diving student needs to do is to become comfortable in the water. By being comfortable I mean that you will need to have some *desire* to know yourself more fully. Without that, there is no need to even be in the water. So let's get into the water.

At this moment, imagine a beautiful Light that looks just like you standing next to you. That would be Me. Now, envision the following scenario: Picture yourself in a swimming pool, a lake, or any body of water in which you feel comfortable. If you are afraid

113

of water, pretend the water is not scary, and tell yourself that this is just an exercise to help you become less afraid of *you*. In your mind, take your time and wade into the water up to your chest. Stay there until you are comfortable with where you are. It is a beautiful day and you are safe. Now look to your left. Floating toward you is a treasure chest that says "Courage." Open this chest and grab all the courage you can, not because you are going into dangerous territory, but because it takes courage to look within. Take this courage and place it in your heart. The beautiful thing about this chest is that the courage inside it already belongs to you. It contains every facet of courage you have ever used to get through your lifetime, starting on the day you were born. Without your realizing it, you already have within you the first step toward diving.

To your right you now can see another chest floating toward you. This one reads "Self-Honesty." Open it and collect every bit of honesty you can muster and place it inside of you. Give yourself permission to be as honest with yourself as you possibly can, for without this, you cannot go any further. Know that, to the left and the right of you, the elements of courage and self-honesty are keeping you afloat. They will neither let you down, nor will they let you sink any further than you desire. And remember, I am still right beside you.

One more chest is floating along, coming your way. This one is labeled "Non-Judgment." Open it with joy and take out every ounce of non-judgment, once again placing the contents within you. This is your safety chest, for it is always easier to feel safer with yourself when you are not judging what you see in the other chests. Courage, self-honesty, and non-judgment are the equipment you will need in order to risk going underwater to open your buried treasure. When you have even the smallest amount of courage to be honest with yourself, and you are willing to give non-judgment a try, allow yourself to sink just under the surface of the water – not too far. Notice that you are able to breathe freely underwater. Look around and realize that here you are, under the water, and nothing bad has happened. All you have to do is enjoy it, knowing that you are safe.

Off in the distance comes a very different looking chest. It is a brilliant, deep azure blue, and as it comes toward you, you see the words "My Strengths." Stay with this chest for a while after you open it. It is very valuable, because it shows you all the wonderful things about yourself that you may have avoided looking at and may have forgotten to remember about yourself. This chest asks you to take an inventory of your life to see how far you have come. Look at and recognize how strong you have been throughout the process of your life. Take notice of your discipline, perseverance, and courage – as well as the compassion, kindness, and love you have given yourself and others. Become aware of your substance as a human being and take the time to acknowledge these qualities that make up who you are. Do not be afraid to appreciate and accept that you are a person of strength. After all, you would not be under the water looking at this chest if you weren't. You may stay under the water with any of these chests for weeks or months. It is all right. Stay as long as you wish, and if you want to come out of the water, do so. When you are ready to go back in, take the four chests with you and ask them to take you a little deeper than before.

This next part of our underwater diving adventure is the most exciting part. You are now ready to dive deeper with courage, self-honesty, non-judgment and strength at your side. Visualize what going deeper means to you, whether you see yourself swimming, diving, or just allowing yourself to sink a bit further into the water. As you feel yourself going to this deeper place, a shimmery silver chest comes to you. On the top are the words "Unflattering Aspects about Myself." This chest is very important to open, Dear One, because until you can see that which you would usually avoid, you cannot move forward in your growth. It is paramount to open this chest and permit yourself to see those unflattering aspects we call "issues," because there is no shame in having them. Everyone does. In fact, you cannot be human without them. Without having "matters of contention" in your life, you would not grow. Opening this chest means that you are willing to look at things you are unhappy about in yourself. This will require *acceptance* that they are a part of who you are until you choose to either work on them or keep them as they are. Either way, being able to acknowledge their existence is the first step. Accepting them is the second, and doing something about them is the third. But for now, use your courage and non-judgment to tolerate opening this chest, because it is a beautiful one. It is the *major* treasure chest that keeps people from diving to their depths. They fear they will see more of what is wrong with them than what is right with them, so they stop diving and get out of the water. This is why it's so important for you to have the right diving gear when you get ready to take the plunge.

I want to make something clear, Dear One, before I talk about our next treasure chest. There is a difference between not liking something about yourself and judging yourself. The first is easier to admit and is bearable because it is natural not to like everything about you. Judging yourself, however, is a choice you make to beat yourself up, which is why you must dive a bit deeper to uncover this formidable chest. If you choose to see what is in this chest, you will find it being drawn to you. As it nears, it reads "Things I Judge About Myself." This is a chest that, when opened, can change your life and the world. In this chest you will explore the myriad of ways by which you punish yourself for those unflattering aspects you just witnessed. You will need to discover why you feel the need to be so hard on yourself. You will have to question why you choose judgment over acceptance. This distinctive chest lies deeper in the water than the others because many of the things one judges about one's self remain hidden.

In general, people think they punish themselves much less than they actually do. Judgment runs rampant in your world. It not only keeps you from feeling deserving of love or whatever it is you want, but it also keeps you judging others. It is this quality that creates distance from others in your life, and creates separation in the human race. I will say more to you about judgment throughout these letters, but for the time being, know that opening this chest is essential to your growth as a human and your evolution as a soul. Hopefully, this is a chest you will continue to open often. It is more than worthy of any attention you can give it, for it is one of the primary keys to discovering your soul.

These various chests, Dear One, will remain with you for the rest of your life. Many more chests make up your buried treasure. I have only mentioned a few important ones, but there are others that need to be opened. You do not have to go to the bottom of the sea and find them all at once. Just find the ones nearest you in everyday life and open them one at a time when you're ready. You will find that, as you become more comfortable in the water, the chests will come to you when you need them. And every chest you open, no matter what it contains, will lead you eventually to the ultimate treasure you seek.

The reward for diving is that, once these chests are open, the contents will no longer be a secret. Your eyes will be opened in a new way, and your newfound awareness will help lessen the fear of knowing yourself more fully. By finding the courage, honesty, and non-judgment to open your buried treasure, you are taking the first step in diminishing the fear of you, thereby lessening the fear of life. This, in itself, is the primary goal of diving: to help you stop being afraid of looking at all of you, so you can swim easily through the water, whether murky or clear. Diving to the depths is a lifetime excursion. It takes time, and if there's anything you have plenty of, Dear One, it is time. So do not be in a hurry. Take things at your own pace so you can learn that the water is not a dangerous place. Rather, know that it is filled with everything you need in order to find love and safety in the world.

Diving to the depths is sacred work because you are a sacred being. It is the depth of self-discovery that will set you free from fear so you can know without a doubt that you have the ability to be your own point of Light in the midst of any darkness you may encounter in your life. By having a closer relationship with yourself, you will one day come upon a solid gold chest adorned with the word "Love." You will know when you are ready to open this chest, and when you do, you will remember that you are not just a presence floating in the ocean of life, you are part of the Ocean itself.

And you will truly believe that all the chests you've worked so hard to open up to this point in time will have been worth it, because you will finally find where God lives – in the depths of your love.

Remaining Stuck: The Fear of Change

Dear One,

It's a funny thing about change. It's the most natural process life has to offer. Once a seedling, the flower transforms itself into a beautiful work of art. The caterpillar emerges as a butterfly. The seasons flow from one to the next. Human beings grow from infancy to adulthood. On your planet everything is in the process of change, including you, whether you can see it or not. Nothing ever remains the same. The difference, however, between you and Nature is that the butterfly cannot choose to remain in the cocoon. The flower cannot choose not to bloom. Winter cannot choose to follow Spring. The only creature on Earth that has the power to create its life with purpose and instigate change is the human being. Yet, fear of change is so great that it not only hinders people from looking within, it also keeps them from moving forward in their lives. It is ironic that the one factor that helps propel human beings toward personal transformation and evolution of consciousness is one of the things they fear the most, *change*.

In your world there is a story about a king who wanted to prove to his people that he was a good king. He decided to choose one person from his kingdom to come and live with him in the castle to give this individual a better life. Certainly, word of this generous offer would spread throughout the land, so his people would know what a beneficent ruler he was. As the king rode out into the countryside, he saw a poor peasant sitting outside his humble hut. This man, the King thought, would be the perfect candidate to receive the gift of a lifetime. Upon bestowing his chivalrous offer to the peasant, with great joy and excitement the peasant agreed to accompany him to the castle. Never in his life did he think a miracle as glorious as this could come his way. But when he straddled the back of the king's horse and they rode on, the peasant began to feel uneasy. As the castle came in view, he became anxious. As the gates opened, the peasant looked back at his home and with panic in his voice cried out, "My hut, my hut."

This, Dear One, is the dilemma that change presents to you in life. Even when it appears that change will be good for you, you may end up stopping your progress because it will mean leaving behind what has always felt comfortable and familiar. If you are not aware of your fear, this kind of security blanket can become your "hut," your crutch. Even if you are courageous enough to leave this familiar hut and venture forth into the unknown, there still will be questions that will evoke your fear of change. "Who will I become if I change? What will happen if I change? Who will be disappointed, angry, or hurt if I change? Who will I lose if I change? What will I have to give up if I change?" These, Dear One, are very good questions, but they also can summon the desire to stay put.

No matter what kind of change you want or are experiencing, whether it is a change of job, of location, of relationship, or a change within you – change will always bring loss. This is the nature of change, and it can be no other way. When you move toward something different in your life, you must leave behind that which was familiar. This is why it is such a powerful fear, and why humans remain stuck in their familiar "huts" rather than venture into the unknown.

There are times when it may seem as if change has thrust itself upon you without your permission. This may feel as if it has come from out of the blue with no rhyme or reason. The truth, more often than not, is that you hear thoughts and have stirrings within you that indicate you may need to make a change in your life. If you do nothing about these cues because you are afraid, the Universe may give you the opportunity to deal with change in a less comfortable way. In fact, it may even feel as though you are being forced to change in order to face your fear, which may be exactly what is happening, not as a punishment, but for your growth. If, as my human counterpart, you have not yet moved toward a soul growth that may be needed, those lessons will find you and will often come in the form of change. This then, gives you the opportunity to work on what you have asked for as a soul, even if you don't remember it, and most likely – you don't.

Recognize, Dear One, that you have the power and the right to change anything you want in your life, including your mind. But when you are stuck in the mindset of "my hut, my hut," remember that you possess all the courage you need to answer to this fear. The doors of change will open time and again throughout your entire life. Taking a risk and leaving your comfort zone to let those doors open will prove to be a rewarding and exhilarating experience if you are willing to embrace change as the positive power it can be. If you can look at change as a way of giving something to yourself, rather than taking something away from yourself, you will have understood more of the beauty and gifts change has to offer.

Keep in mind that love sustains all things, including change. Love for yourself and love from Me will help you endure any kind of change. However, diminishing your fear of change will require a change of residence for you, Dear One. It will mean saying good bye to your hut. It will mean getting on the horse with Me to head for a better life. Know, without doubt, that I will always lead the way and take us in the right direction. Do not be afraid. The riches in the castle await you. It's okay if you don't always believe in this kind of fairy tale. I have enough belief for the two of us.

There's a Little Tarnish on Everybody's Halo: The Fear of Not Being Good Enough

Dear One,

You live in a world that constantly touts perfection: the perfect weight, the perfect skin, the perfect age, the perfect body, the perfect grade in school. As a result, people are reminded on a daily basis of how flawed they are and that they do not measure up to the standard your world sees as "perfect." This creates within the self a sense of not being good enough. Add to this your personal experiences of how you felt about yourself in your family of origin, how you were treated and accepted by your teachers and peers in school, and what you were taught by your religious culture about your lovability and deservedness. Is it any surprise that most people suffer from the ingrained belief that they are not good enough? These feelings are like an underlying river that flows through every human being at one time or another. They affect one's feelings of desirability and worth. Not feeling good enough may not prevail as a conscious thought, but believe me, it is hiding somewhere within most people.

Therefore, many people in your world suffer from the expectation that in order to be good enough they have to be perfect. In fact, some believe that to be spiritual one must strive for perfection. Although the desire to better one's self is a wonderful thing, striving for perfection can only result in disappointment, because it is unattainable.

Know, without a doubt, Dear One, that you did not come here to be perfect, nor does God expect perfection from you. Rather, you are meant to be in process. You are here to make mistakes. Blunders, botches, and bungles are all part of growth. In fact, you cannot evolve without them. You are perfectly imperfect. Part of being human is accepting that everyone has issues, insecurities, and negativity. However, it is not the issues, insecurities, or negativity that cause the problem of believing you are not good enough. It is the *judgments* you carry about the issues, insecurities, and negativity that weigh you down. The more judgment you place on yourself for not being good enough, the heavier the burden you carry.

It is also not a sin to believe that you *are* good enough. This doesn't mean that you don't desire to be more than who you are now. It simply means that you are willing to lovingly give yourself permission to accept who you are, warts and all, despite the fact that you may not be where you want to be in life. This is good enough. This is acceptance. When you can create within yourself an atmosphere of acceptance of who you are right now, you will allow yourself to create the space for self-respect and love of self.

Lessening the fear of not feeling good enough will require the recognition that you are not here to follow anyone else's path but your own. Human beings have a tendency to look up to and compare themselves to the people they admire. When you compare yourself to another, you set yourself up to fall short, and it can only lead you to the place of not feeling good enough. Remember that you are not here to be someone else or to live up to someone else's standard. You have come into this life with your own areas of soul growth, your own specific purpose, your own unique energy package, and your own marvelous journey. Consequently, if you have chosen to bring into this lifetime the ingredients for being a carrot cake, stop trying to be a stew! You are as God made you, using the potential He gave you. How can you be more "good enough" than that?

Therefore, Dear One, know that I am not here to assist you in moving toward perfection. You are already that in the spiritual sense because you are Me. I am here to help you accept your human imperfection and embrace it as a stepping stone to seeing the spiritual perfection you already are. In other words, during this lifetime, you will wear the halo of a Divine Being living in human form. But you must also accept the tarnish of imperfection that comes with being human. Everyone is born good enough. When you believe this with all your heart, then you will lead a successful life, for that is the true meaning of success. Leading a fulfilling life comes from the realization that you don't have to prove yourself to anyone. For better or for worse, you are "imperfectly" beautiful, just because you are you.

Therefore, Dear One, realize that perfection is an illusion of your human existence. You are not required to be perfect for yourself, for another, or for God. Your value is as great as it is *ever* going to be. You are never going to be any more valuable than you are right now in this very moment. No matter what you do in life, no matter how many people you affect in your work, no matter how successful you become – you are no more valuable now than the day you were born. Your worth was already determined the moment God breathed life into you. Therefore, the ultimate truth is that there is no such thing as not being good enough. Once again, it is only your lack of belief in yourself that makes it so.

Staying Small: The Fear of What Others Think

Dear One,

All children seek the approval of their parents. It is part of the process of being a child. A parent's approval gives a child its first inklings of self-esteem, value, and love. However, when the tables are turned and a child receives disapproval from one or both parents, albeit unintentional, a child can equate this with rejection. Then, in order to feel lovable and loved once more, a child's natural tendency will be to solicit even more attention and approval, not only from its parents, but from others as well. For most people, this need for approval continues even after they "grow up" and often for the rest of their lives.

This particular dynamic easily links itself to one of Mankind's most commonplace fears. The fear of what others think may appear minor and subtle, but it packs a powerful wallop when activated, so do not underestimate its influence. It can deter people from following their chosen path in life. It can keep love from finding its way to another and can hold unhappy, mismatched relationships together to struggle onward. It keeps politicians from honoring their promises and doing what is right, for fear of violating party ties. It inhibits honesty and authenticity toward oneself and others. Fearing what others think can be so ingrained that many people do not even recognize it as a problem. In fact, some view it as admirable by confusing it with the mindset that the opinions of others are always valuable. Note that I do not mean *considering* what others think.

I am speaking of the *fear* of what others think, which is distinctly different. Considering what others think can be a wonderful way of reaching consensus and learning about yourself. It is part of becoming a mature human being. But the fear of what others think is altogether a different animal. It has the potential to create a lifetime of worry and immobility because it is closely connected to the fear of not being liked.

I am not saying there is anything wrong with wanting to be liked. Most people want to be liked. It's natural. The challenge occurs when *wanting* to be liked turns into *needing* to be liked. Dear One, there was a time in your life when I watched you dim your own beautiful Light because what others thought of you was more important than what you thought of yourself. Society had taught you that feeling good about yourself remained in the hands of other people. Therefore, in order to ensure that you felt valued and loved, you believed that you had to please everyone. Hence, you grew into a young woman who did not rock any boat, kept her anger and disappointment with others a secret, and decided that she had better not have too many differing opinions. In effect, you put others above yourself and made the choice to stay small.

The fear of what others think is prevalent in your world because of the fear of rejection felt by the inner child's fear of disapproval long ago. Being rejected and the ensuing loss pose an immense risk for most people, which is why the fear of rejection remains so widespread. The price paid for succumbing to this fear is enormous, because you end up losing yourself. When the thoughts of what others think of you carry more clout than what you think of yourself, you have just placed others on the top rung of your emotional ladder. In doing so, you have lowered yourself to a bottom rung and placed yourself in a lesser position, one of smallness.

The paradox surrounding this is that no matter how much approval you receive from others, unless you have resolved your own fear of rejection, you will never believe the words of approval you do get. If you do not believe in yourself, believing the good things someone else says about you will always have a limited shelf life. In many a mind lurks the thought, "If they *really* knew me they probably wouldn't like me, because *I* don't like me." With that thought comes the following vicious cycle: You fear what others think because you fear their rejection, which causes you to withhold your thoughts and feelings in order to win their approval. Then, when and if you do get their approval, you don't believe it because you haven't accepted what you don't like about yourself. This leads you back to depending on them for approval all over again.

I know you are aware of this principle, Dear One, and that it no longer plays a predominant role in your life. Nevertheless, it is important to reiterate the impact of this fear not only for the reader, but also for you, because this particular fear has the potential to raise its head time and again after these letters are published.

There is good news about the fear of what others think, because there is a remedy. It is a simple countermeasure that with practice becomes much easier to execute. The antidote is that you must give *everyone* permission not to like you. If it is okay for you not to like everyone, then it be must be okay that not everyone likes you. You can scurry around in your head trying to figure out why someone may not like you, but you may never know why, so it doesn't matter. There will always be someone in your life that you do not like, and there will always be someone who does not like you. And you must make that okay.

By giving *yourself* permission not to like everything about you, you give others the same permission. In other words, why should people like everything about you when *you* don't like everything about you? When you can accept that it is all right for others to think what they will, you give yourself the precious opportunity to let go of the fear of what they think. Then, because you have given them permission to think as they wish, they can no longer hold any power over you. When you are no longer fearful in this way, what they think of you will then become none of your business. And that, Dear One, is a wonderful thing.

Bear in mind that no matter what anyone thinks of you, you are not responsible for anyone else's thoughts, notions, or conjectures. Whatever thoughts one may have, the responsibility for those thoughts resides within that individual. If others judge you, either openly or in their thoughts, this also is not about you. The judgment cast is on their karmic plate, not yours, and this is also none of your business. Their karma is *their* karma. The same applies to any judgments you may hold about others.

Of course, you are going to care most about those you like or love and what they think of you. It is important to listen to their perceptions of you, because they may see something in you that you are unable to see in yourself. No one can be totally objective about himself or herself. Therefore, be open to their opinions about you and thank them for pointing out what you may not have been able to see. This will enhance your growth. However, if you have looked deeply within yourself and do not agree, it is equally important to remember that you are the sole judge of how well you know yourself. When you truly believe that you know yourself better than anyone else does, it is all right to accept or reject another's version of who you are. By saying, "I accept that what you are saying is your truth about me, but it is not *my* truth about me," you are showing respect for yourself, as well as for the other person.

You, and you alone, are responsible for what you think about yourself – and you, and you alone, are responsible for your own approval or rejection. When you give yourself the gift of honest appraisal and approval, you will let go of the fear that insists you need others to make you feel worthy, lovable, and good enough.

As you know, Dear One, this kind of inner work takes courage and determination, and it is exactly this path of knowing yourself that is the panacea for helping heal your world. Any reduction of fear in an individual life will inevitably help reduce fear in the world, and right now your world needs a little help in that department. So I say this to you with love: Allow boats to rock, opinions to flow, and thoughts and feelings to be expressed. You are part of the Source that created you, and you did not come here to stay small. You came to let your Light shine, and by allowing your Light to show its own unique brilliance, you also give others permission to do the same.

There Are No Bad Marks on Your God Card: The Fear of God

Dear One,

When babies are born, they have the full remembrance of God. They remember where they came from and who they are as a soul. It may appear that they are a blank slate, but they are not. They carry a consciousness so profound that you can get a glimpse of it if you look closely enough. In fact, if you have ever looked deeply into a baby's eyes, as those eyes look back at you it is quite obvious that this tiny being is more aware than you might think. As babies evolve into young children, the awe, wonder, and joy they exhibit is clearly the remembrance of God in full bloom. This awareness of knowing you are part of the Creator continues throughout the lifetime of every human being, for the soul never forgets. As the child develops, however, forgetting the eternal Home begins to take place within his or her human personality. This is what I call "the fall." It is not a fall from grace. It is the fall from remembering to forgetting which every soul must experience while in physical form in order to continue its evolution.

Although as a young child you remembered your God within, as you grew older you were taught many things about God that you did not understand. You learned fairly quickly that the pastor who stood above everyone at his pulpit had a more direct line to God than anyone else. He was a nice man and you liked him, but as you listened year after year about who God was supposed to be, you had the feeling that something wasn't quite right. The God you remembered did not match what you were being told. You thought it must be your fault because who were *you* to know anything about God? Consequently, the joyful, loving God you once believed Him to be gradually went from a flame to an ember because you came to fear God.

From the beginning of your religious education you were taught that the first humans created by God were a terrible disappointment. God gave them everything, but then in a garden one day curiosity got the best of them and they disobeyed Him. From then on, they ruined it for everybody, including you. Now you were supposedly born of sin because of their huge mistake. As a child you wondered, "How is that fair?" Since you were also taught that God expected you to forgive, you could not understand why He didn't.

You learned that not only was God unforgiving, but He was also jealous. So you wondered, "What could God be jealous of if He can have anything and everything He wants?" These teachings did not help you feel closer to God, Dear One. Instead, they made your fear of Him increase. It was when you learned that God was vengeful that you totally forgot the God you once knew. The stories you heard about God's "wrath," in which He was angry and quick to punish, frightened you even more. Although your pastor was not a "hell and brimstone" kind of preacher, it was still made known that if you did not live by the rules God set forth, you could be sent to a burning fire called Hell, where you would live to be tortured eternally with all the other "bad" people. Even when it was revealed that God loved you so much that He sent His only son to be sacrificed to grant you everlasting life, you were not comforted. Not only did you surmise that God had a favorite child (which wasn't you, by the way), but you also felt guilty that His only son had to die so horribly. And your little mind wondered, "How could a loving Father allow this to happen?"

When you grew into an older child, you accepted the teachings of the church without question. As you watched the congregation leave each service, shaking hands with the pastor and looking happy, you wondered, "Why are they so happy?" After being told quite often that you were not worthy of being in the presence of the Lord, all you felt was inadequate, unworthy, and sinful. What made you happy was going home. Maybe that's what they were happy about, too, you thought. It is not My intent, Dear One, to demean yours or anyone's experience of religion. It is My desire to help you examine this fundamental fear and where it came from. While as a child you liked the music, ritual, and socialization of going to church, its teachings affected you more than you could have known. You are not alone, for there is a multitude of others who have been affected in the same way.

Your impression of who God is worsened as time went on and you became a young adult. You learned that God could not only be jealous, loving, and vengeful, but also unpredictable. At a moment's notice, He could take your life because He needed you. It seemed that when anyone died of anything other than old age, you were told that God needed them, and that's why they were taken. You wondered, "If, as the hymns announce, that God is Lord of all Lords and King of all Kings, what could He possibly need from this person or this child?" This not only instilled in you a fear that you could be next on His list, but if He did take you, would He be disappointed if you were not able to give Him what He needed?

With all this in mind you continued to ask the man in the pulpit for guidance, and you were finally given the answers that would help you give God what He wanted. First, you needed to worship and adore him, and put no one else above Him. Second, you must love Him with all your heart, soul, and mind. Third, you must fear Him – and this you did, Dear One, for many young years. Because you were told that God knows every thought you have, you thought

132

He would know that you did not love Him in the way you were supposed to. You were too afraid of God to really love Him. With this recognition came incredible guilt and fear, so much so that the majority of your youth was spent trying to prove that you were good.

I am here to set the record straight, Dear One. Although I do not have the language to adequately describe who God is, I do know how to tell you who God is not. I say this to you with all My heart, soul, and mind: With the exception of loving you unconditionally, God is none of the above. You were taught wrong. There was never anything sinful about you, nor can there ever be. This is because you are, God is, and you and God are One. You were created through love, and God will never rescind that love.

Throughout time, Mankind has tried to understand who God is. Since God is indescribable to humans, in order to identify with and connect to Him, men chose to see God as an extension of Mankind. This was the only way they knew how to relate to God at the time. In this way, men made God in their own image. But it is Man, not God, who is vengeful, judgmental, angry, and jealous. It is Man who is punishing, unforgiving, unpredictable, and unjust. It is Man who to this very day condemns and kills others in the name of God. And it is Man who has stopped trusting in his own goodness and Godness.

Therefore, there are no bad marks on your God card, Dear One. No matter how many mistakes you make, no matter what you do with your life, you cannot offend God. You did not come to this Earth to atone for your "badness." Instead, God has given you the opportunity to use your free will to remember who you are and to develop at your own pace. He gives you as many chances as you need to know that He is within you. This is what real love is like, and the reason it is sometimes so hard to believe it is that most humans rarely experience a love such as this.

Because it is important, I will say this to you again. You cannot offend God. Don't you think by now that God has had reason enough to be offended by centuries of Mankind's antics – and yet He does nothing? People continue to wonder, "Why isn't He saving the world? Why isn't He punishing the 'evil' ones, and why isn't He showing Himself to make people believe that He exists?" Here is your answer, Dear One. The reason God does not show up and reveal His Presence to the world is because He is already here! He is here in each one of you. It is up to all of you to make the changes you want to see in the world. Through His love for you, He has given you the opportunity lifetime after lifetime to make changes in your world. Change, however, cannot occur until people begin to recognize that they have the God-given power within themselves to create their lives and their world in the manner they want. This power cannot be fully recognized until love of self is sought. Once you gain love of self, you will intrinsically feel love for others. It is then your world will change. Can you see how the future of your world depends on every human being making a change from fear to love?

God's greatest joy would be for you to know yourself as the powerful Creator you are, to believe that you can create anything you want, including a new world, and to love yourself and others the way He loves you. *Your* greatest joy can be that He loves you enough to wait until you come to that conclusion yourself. And you will one day. Everyone will in their right and perfect time, when they make the choice to do so.

Therefore, rather than seeing God as ready to judge you, think of Him as the father of the prodigal who sends one of his sons into the world to make a fortune for the family. When the son returns home ashamed of squandering all of the money, his father does not rebuke him. Instead, he embraces his son with as much love as he bestows on his other children. God is the Father who sends all of you into the world to make your own decisions and to make your fortune as you wish. There is no judgment. There is no offense taken. There is only Love. You will *all* be welcomed Home with open arms. As much as there are many who may not want to believe this because of their own judgmental and punishing natures, there are no exceptions. This is the true story of who God is.

Yes, Dear One, you will make mistakes and you will face the consequences of your actions through the universal laws of karma and cause and effect. You will work on soul growth lessons until you no longer need to do so. But you will not be judged or punished by God. Rather, because you have the gift of free will, it will be you who will decide how to answer to your own fate. And you will answer out of love, not fear. This is why you have eternity to play out your individual and collective issues. And you have the same eternity to enjoy the journey along the way.

I also want to say to you and to anyone else who has feared God: Know that the only Devil who's out to get you is your own negativity. Know that this cosmic bogeyman has never existed, except in your mind. Know that it is impossible for an angelic being filled with God's love to have the desire to leave God's side or to fall from the sky or anywhere else. There is no such thing as a fallen angel who creates evil in your world. Instead, know that it is the collective negative energy of Man, and nothing else, that has created the space for hatred in your world. There are no evil souls, only human beings who have totally forgotten who they are. And out of such darkness comes evil. Forgive them, for they know not what they do.

You do have a Father who, through His love for you, will welcome you Home no matter what. Know that His Divine Presence of Love resides in you through Me. Therefore, God is always with you. In your persistence to find yourself, you have bumped into the God within. By doing so you have helped the child within to remember the God she once knew. She no longer lies awake fearing that someday she will be punished for her "badness." Now she sleeps soundly in My arms, knowing she is safe and loved. Thank you, Dear One, for giving her that gift, and for giving it to yourself. And thank you for giving others the opportunity to know the truth of who God really is: the Presence of Unconditional and Abiding Love.

If I'm Too Happy: The Fear of Happiness

Dear One,

One of the treasure chests you found years ago while diving to your depths was "The Fear of Being Too Happy." Because you are one who generally gravitates toward the positive, it took you time to realize that this fear was, indeed, a part of you. As you soon discovered, the day your mother whispered to you "Don't tell anyone we're moving" was a day that changed your life and created your fear of being too happy. As a five year old, you had no idea what your mother meant when she said those words, other than that you and your family were about to leave your current residence. Then, as the moving van pulled out of the driveway with only you, your brother, and your mother, you realized that your father was not coming. There was no warning, no goodbye. One day you were a happy five-year-old, and the next you were thrust into a world of loss, confusion, and fear. Not only was it momentous because you lost the only world you had ever known, but also because, unknowingly, you made one of the biggest decisions of your life. You decided you could never be totally happy again. This decision became a core belief within you, and as the loss of your father became more evident, it gained even greater validation and momentum. The belief that you could never be too happy, for fear that something out of the blue might suddenly take it away, gradually sank into the depths of your psyche. Once there, it found its way into one of your treasure chests, to be hidden away for years to come. This does not mean that you resigned yourself to a life of misery. You did not. There were still happy moments and happy times, but you lacked the essence of pure joy, Dear One.

As the years wore on, your little mind thought that because something bad had happened to you, *you* must be bad. You thought that bad things only happened to bad people, so God must have wanted it this way. What you did next was actually quite ingenious for a child. You thought that if *you* were to abandon your own happiness before God or anything else did, then *you* would be the one in control of not having other bad things happen. It was your way of saying, "Look God, I'm already unhappy, so find somebody else to bother." You thought you needed to beat God to the punch before He made more bad things come your way. If you could show God that you were already suffering, then He might take pity on you, pass you by, and leave you alone. And the only way you knew how to show God that you were suffering was to not allow yourself to be boundlessly happy, at least not for too long. You don't remember this thought process, but it was there. It was how you learned to cope. Every child finds his or her own way to handle life's difficult situations, and this was yours. Although I continued to whisper to you over the years that it's okay to have a totally happy day, your core belief at that time was too strong to hear My words.

I know that revealing this is personal and somewhat uncomfortable for you, Dear One. However, it is important because many who read this book will see that they, too, are fearful of being overly happy. They will also recognize how joy has eluded them. Their stories may vary, but the happiness theme will remain the same. There will also be others who may realize that they have unwittingly made childhood decisions that last for a lifetime. Therefore, Dear One, it is with love that I use your experience as My example.

I know that you no longer protect yourself from being happy the way you did as a child. However, I want to point out to you and others that, because it is a core belief, this fear does not easily go away. It is so ingrained that sometimes you can forget to see its persistent nuances in your present day life. I say this to you so you can become more aware of how it can subtly slip back into your psyche. For example, have you noticed at times when you are feeling really happy how a negative thought can suddenly pop into your mind for no apparent reason? One minute you feel great, and the next minute that feeling has disappeared. Where did it go? What happened? I will tell you what happened. You created the negative thought to come into your mind in order to protect you from feeling too happy. This is your ever familiar and habitual fear coming back for a visit.

It is also important to be aware that your fear of being too happy can come about in your conversations with others. For example, when you were finished building your house a few years ago you were asked, "How do you like your new home?" You replied, "It's nice, but what a difficult time we had building it." Another friend asked, "How was your vacation?" You answered, "It was good, but too short and it rained for four days." Starting sentences with a positive thought and ending them with a negative one is a good way to keep happiness at bay. Therefore, exit joy. Although this is not an example of a direct fear that something bad will happen, it still conveys your child's underlying need to protect herself from being happy. You see, Dear One, this is how the five-year-old's promise to herself can still come into play.

Awareness will always be the key to reversing any belief. The more cognizant you are of your feelings, thoughts, and dialogues, the more able you will be to change your fear of being too happy. It is a wonderful thing to watch you now exclaiming, "My house is wonderful. I love it! My vacation was exactly what I needed! I'm doing great! My life is good!" So much has changed in your life since you've allowed yourself to be happy without fear. Know that I do not expect you to be happy all the time. No one is. Everyone has unhappy moments, because at times life can certainly be a struggle. Also recognize, however, that there are times when life purposely becomes a struggle when it doesn't have to be.

Not everyone reading this letter will connect with the fear of being too happy. However, I can tell you with certainty that millions of people in your world will continue to use unhappiness as a crutch. You live in a Society that is addicted to suffering. Without being aware, most human beings will habitually look for ways to be upset, angry, and unhappy, for negative ego takes pleasure in suffering negative emotions. The drama of being unhappy is much more appealing and exciting to the ego than being happy or peaceful. No matter whether it's TV drama, life's drama, or world drama, it titillates the ego and dispels boredom. There is an unconscious pleasure that comes with negativity. Therefore, without realizing it, most people get something out of being unhappy.

Some will not allow themselves happiness because others in the world are suffering. They feel they don't have a right to be totally happy when other people are worse off than they are. Many believe suffering is necessary as a way of atoning for sin. Others are unhappy because it is the only way they can get attention and sympathy. They fear being cast aside if they exhibit their happiness. Some people use unhappiness as a currency to pay for feelings of guilt, or as a punishment for a crime they think they have committed. And of course, happiness will always take a back seat if one is intent on being a victim, because victims cannot be happy. Otherwise, they couldn't be victims anymore. Last but not least, there will always be those who believe their happiness is someone else's responsibility, not their own. Therefore, they can't be happy until they have someone else's permission to be so.

The truth of the matter, Dear One, is that happiness is a choice. It is a decision that says you can be happy where you are standing right now. Happiness is *your* responsibility and you have the ability to create it, anytime and anywhere. Know that you do not have to be intent on gathering *more* happiness in your life. You are here on this Earth to *deepen* your experience of happiness, because it is your birthright. You have the right to be happy.

Over the last sixty years I have watched you grow and relinquish much of your childhood decision. I have witnessed the consistent happiness you have gradually allowed into your life. I have observed your willingness to release a magnificent jubilance into the world. In essence, I have watched you remember who you really are, and it brings Me great joy. Every time you feel that inner smile of joy, Dear One, you are feeling Me shining my Light through you, waiting with excitement and anticipation for your next happy thought, your next happy moment, and your next happy day. In these happy moments, try to remind yourself that this is who you really are, a joyous soul creating an extraordinary life.

Going Home: The Fear of Death

Dear One,

In your dream you were a bride standing at the altar with your husband-to-be, about to take your marital vows. At that moment you realized that you must be dreaming, because you knew you would never marry this particular man in "real life." With a smile on your face, you turned to the congregation and said, "Thank you for coming, everyone, but this is just a dream. Come outside and I will show you." Your guests exited the church, wondering what you were going to do next. When they had assembled outside, you looked at them and said, "I am going to prove to you that this is just a dream. Watch me – I can fly!" Without hesitation, you leaped into the air and took off as the onlookers below stood aghast. You flew in circles and figure eights and performed all kinds of loop-de-loops. You were ecstatic that you could, at will, determine what your next acrobatic aerial move was going to be.

The scene suddenly changed, and you found yourself in the driver's seat of a car. Instinctively, you placed your arms in front of you in a flying position and, freely exiting through the windshield, in a brilliant flash of light you left the car. In an instant, you found yourself flying over beautiful countryside. Gazing below, you saw farms and noticed that there was snow on the ground. At first, you wondered where you were, but in your excitement, wonder, and freedom, you decided that it really didn't matter. You flew for a moment longer, and then, as you slowly woke up, you remembered that you were in

Midland, Texas and it was late September. You were hoping today would be in the low eighties like yesterday, so you could sit by the pool. As you lay in bed, you thought about the dream and told your husband how extraordinary it had been. The feeling of freedom had been unlike anything you had ever experienced. As your soul-mate got out of bed to begin his day, he called you to come and look out the window. And there it was – an inch of snow on the ground from a freak storm that had found its way to Texas that morning!

Dear One, what I want to say to you is that, with the exception of being totally detached from your body, you were having the death experience. You left the denseness of your physical body behind and moved into your light body. You became free, boundless, and able to move at will. By seeing the dream of snow while in your light body before actually seeing it in your physical body, you were finally able to grasp that you were not just of this world. You knew without doubt you that are able to exist outside of the physical realm and experience yourself in another dimension.

Death is very much like your flying dream. It is a transition from the density of the human body to the lightness of the etheric body. You retain all consciousness, yet vibrate at a much higher frequency. You continue to live, Dear One. Think of it in this Zen-like way: When water boils, it continues to live as steam. When a cloud bursts, it continues to live as rain. When wood burns, it continues to live as smoke. When you die, you continue to live through Spirit, the Light vibration you have always been. In other words, you keep on going, even though the temporary play is over. You end one chapter of your life to go on to the next. You open one door to move through another. Death is just another beginning, Dear One, not an end. You simply change residence.

In the course of a lifetime, you go through many "little deaths," or transitions. Every time you move through another stage of life, you experience a death. Whenever you conquer a fear, you experience a death. Physical death, however, is not only the final one, it is the best one. I am not talking about the dying process, rather about the death experience when you, as Me, will leave the physical body and transition to the other side.

Just as life has its own process, so does death. It is important for you to know that no one ever dies alone. Your Spirit Guides, who have never left your side, will be there, and when you see them you will recognize them immediately. Angelic forces and your own Guardian Angel will also be there to escort you Home. No one comes into this life alone, and no one leaves it alone. So do not think you will be left to float around willy-nilly by yourself. You will not. Quite possibly, you will recognize someone who has gone before you, someone you love and miss who will also be there to escort you Home. This loved one will be there to give you the comfort of knowing that you are going to a safe place. Your most profound moment of death will be the overwhelming feeling of love you will immediately know to be the Presence of God. At this moment you will remember the feeling of Home. I tell you these things so you will know what to expect when you are fully Me.

When you take your last Earthly breath you will be totally conscious and able to see everything and everyone around you, including the body you just left behind. You may decide to stay in this space a little while longer so you can be with family and friends and send them your love. But you will soon be ready to move forward with the realization that they are not gone from you. They may feel as if they have lost you, but you will know differently. However, you *will* leave many things behind. You will leave behind all that you have had to contend with during your life on Earth. You will bid farewell to worry, struggle, responsibilities, and pain. You will no longer be concerned with anything of the material world. It will not matter how much money is in the bank, what people say, how much your body weighed, or who did what to whom. None of this will have any significance for you.

Your death will become more apparent to you when you meet up with those who have loved and cared about you and are waiting for your return. When this "grand reunion" (as it is called) begins, not only will you see those you knew from this lifetime, but those from other lives as well – for they will recognize you by your vibrational energy, your spiritual fingerprint, if you will. In essence, although you will still have the physical appearance of the life you have just left, they will know you and welcome you Home.

Your spiritual mentor used to say that going from the dense body into the light body is like going beyond gravity into space. This is true. Therefore, you will need a time of rest to adjust to the lightness of your new body. During this time you will become acclimated to your new energy and will receive the blessings, love, and prayers of those on the Earthly level as well as those from this realm. It will be like stopping at an inn to rest for the night before continuing on your journey.

It is during this time of rest and adjustment that you are given the opportunity to look at your life from the moment of your birth to your death. This is literally your lifetime in review. You will have total recall of your purpose for reincarnating. You will be able to understand the cast of characters in your play, both ally and villain, and how they fit into your life. And as you look back at your life, Dear One, you will feel no judgment from yourself or others because you will no longer have an ego that needs to criticize and scold. Judgment is a product of Man's world, not God's.

I also want you to know that there will never be a time when the Creator pronounces some of his children guilty and the rest innocent. The Almighty leaves the details up to you, which is why karma and soul growth are put into place at the beginning of Earthly life. You as a soul, not God, will determine how well you have followed the agenda you set forth. And whether you did or not won't matter, because you will understand what kept you from remembering while you were here. With that knowledge will come compassion and love for who you were in that lifetime and who you are now as a soul. You must always remember, Dear One, that in the world of the Divine love always prevails, because love is all there is.

As you begin to see with your spiritual eyes – in actuality, My eyes – you will understand yourself in a way you never have before. You will have full comprehension of why you were the way you were. You will have a new understanding of the positive and negative impact you had on others and the impact they had on you. You will realize how well you were able to give love to yourself and others, and how able you were to receive it. You will have total remembrance that you came from a spiritual place and are returning to that spiritual space. Everything will finally make sense, and you will feel Oneness with all things once again.

This may be very difficult for some to believe because it sounds too good to be true. Yet, how could God create anything else but this? Why wouldn't the spiritual place from whence you came be so much more than what you've ever known in the physical lifetime? Why wouldn't your existence as a soul be greater than your existence as a human? And why wouldn't the love that is waiting for you be more magnificent than any love you have ever experienced on Earth?

Only fear can keep one from believing this. Fear of death causes more angst in your world than death itself, because people fear what they do not understand. And because humans are preoccupied with their physical bodies, they fear that when they lose their bodies upon death, they will also lose who they are. So you see, Dear One, what I call "graduation," and what you call death, is not to be feared. Death is actually a rebirth. You change form. You change costume. The play ends and you go Home to write yet another play.

But even as I tell you this, I am sensing a sadness within. I can feel a melancholy you have about leaving this particular lifetime behind. The thought of losing your husband feels like more than

146

you can bear. I tell you this, Dear One. You never lose anyone. Ever. Either you will be waiting for him when he arrives Home, or he will be waiting for you. Love cannot be separated, only found and re-discovered. All those you have loved will be waiting for you when you cross over.

Let me reassure you as well that even though you are My human personality, you are not going to be left behind either. You are coming with Me. I will bring the beauty of you with Me. I will bring all the memories of love you have ever given and received, and every kindness you have ever bestowed. I will bring all the best of this recent lifetime together with the best of every lifetime I have ever lived, so that the vastness of you will continue to grow through Me. Death is only a dimension, not an ending. So when I leave this world, your essence will come with Me. As I become all of who I am, you will always be with Me. You will be a most beautiful thread of Light in the tapestry of My existence.

When you meet your death, Dear One, it will be like waking up from a dream. You will realize that the Earth experience was the dream, and where you are now is the reality. While you were dreaming, it seemed so real. Yet, in the grand scheme of things it lasted only seconds. Death is your awakening from the dream. There is nothing to fear. Just picture yourself in the driver's seat of a car. Together we will put our arms out ready to soar, and then freely and easily, we will exit the windshield of your body in a most brilliant flash of light, ready to go Home – joyously looking forward to our next adventure, whatever and wherever that might be.

Section V:

Open These Letters When You Want to Remember Love of Self

The Point of No Return

Dear One,

There comes a time in life when you love someone so deeply that you know you have passed the point of no return. There is no turning back. Without exception, you know you will love this person forever, no matter what they say or do. They can hurt you or even leave you, but no matter how hard you might try, you cannot stop loving them. This does not mean that this relationship will remain intact, or that you will ever see each other again. It means that this person will always hold a special place in your heart, because love can never be annulled. Loving someone past the point of no return is unconditional and eternal. It is the kind of love most people wish for. This is the love I feel for you and the love I wish for all human beings to have in their lives. When you can love *yourself* past the point of no return, you will have found the key to changing yourself and your world from a place of fear to a place of love.

There is something about love that most people do not comprehend. They think of love as a human quality. But it is not. It is a spiritual quality that expresses itself through the human heart. Love is the essence of God that souls bring with them when they come to the Earth plane. Therefore, any time you love anything or anyone, you are experiencing your own Divinity. To go one step further, whenever you want love in your life, it really means that you want to reconnect with the unconditional love you knew before you got here. In essence, the "real you," your soul, longs to connect with

God. Because you were born of that love, Dear One, you want to feel it as fully as you can. Since you feel it less when in human form, you seek it all the more. In order to experience loving yourself past the point of no return, you will need to find this kind of love within yourself.

Loving yourself is the foundation from which all good things come. How much you love yourself will determine how much you love others. The degree to which you love others will determine how much peace exists in your world. And how much peace exists in the world will determine the survival of your planet. When you do not give thought to loving yourself, there is a tendency to forget who you really are. When you forget who *you* are, you then forget who everyone else is. In that forgetfulness, the belief that you are separate from everything and everyone continues to produce much suffering in your world. I tell you this, Dear One, because the greatest challenge of your time is not war, the economy, job loss, poverty, or racism. It is the perpetuation of the deeply rooted lack of love for oneself that creates these devastating conditions. It is loving the self that is going to change your world; yet ironically, it is the last place most people look for love.

Loving yourself is a spiritual act like no other. When you love yourself, you are loving God. When you refuse to love yourself, you refuse to love God. It is as simple as that. For how can you say you love God, but not love yourself, when you are One and the same? There are those who say, "This is not true. I can still love God and not love myself. I pray every day. I worship God every Sunday. I live my life for God." I must tell you, Dear One, that this is not what loving God is all about. It is what you have been taught to believe it is all about. Prayer and gratefulness are certainly part of loving God, but the best way to know and love God is to spend time focusing on loving yourself.

Many believe that loving yourself is a self-centered act that is equated with selfishness and vanity. They think it is characterized by bragging to others about how great you are when you are not. This is not self-love. Loving the self is expressed through compassion, respect, trust, understanding, and non-judgment. When you love who you are, you have the ability and desire to share your love and give it away. In other words, loving yourself is not something to be contained. Rather, you ultimately expand the love you feel for yourself to others, because you have more than enough to go around. When you truly love yourself, you are able to take love beyond yourself, for such expansion is at the heart of love.

When the Great Master said, "Love thy neighbor as thyself," he knew you could not truly love others until you first had an inherent love for yourself. He knew that loving yourself would lead to feeling the love of God within. Once that was felt, you would then remember not only your own core nature, but also the core nature of all others. It is interesting that in your world this particular phrase is used much more frequently as an indication to put others before you more so than as a reminder that loving yourself is just as important as loving others.

It may seem as though loving yourself is an insurmountable task, but it is not. Dear One, let me remind you that you have all of eternity to work on this. For this lifetime, I will point you in the right direction in the remaining letters. One important thought to remember during this process is this: just as fear is a river with many tributaries, so is love.

One of the greatest tributaries of love is acceptance. If you want to experience love for who you are, acceptance must be part of your repertoire. You must start with accepting who you are right now. This does not mean you have to like everything about yourself. It means that you must be willing to acknowledge your strengths as well as your weaknesses, the latter without self-judgment. Acceptance is a tributary of love based on who you are now, rather than on who you want to be, or who you pretend to be. If you want to be more than who you are now, then you can move toward that path, but unconditional love for who you are right now is imperative.

The difficult question that needs to be asked by those willing to undertake this venture is: Can you love yourself even though you are not yet all you want to be? Can you still feel love for yourself despite that which is not lovable about you? Can you feel enough love for yourself that you know there is no going back? Can you betray yourself, and still feel love for who you are? Ultimately, Dear One, can you pass the point of no return with yourself? In your willingness to say, "Yes, I accept that I am not yet who I want to be, but I am working on ridding myself of self judgment and replacing it with acceptance and compassion," then you are taking a crucial step toward self-love.

Loving yourself is a feeling of joy like no other. Whenever you love *you*, you automatically feel the connection with Me, which gives you the confidence that you are alright, now and always. It is a profound love that emanates from within, a glow that insists you are glad you are *you* and no one else. It is a mindset that says, "I am what I am, and I will be the best me I can be – not according to a checklist or anyone else's expectations, but based on how I feel about myself." When you have passed the point of no return with yourself, Dear One, you are feeling a smidgeon of what God feels like.

From the moment you were created, God has loved you past the point of no return. When you can think of yourself the way God thinks of you and can feel the way God feels about you – and when you can treat yourself the way you think God would treat you – you will love yourself past the point of no return. If you can continue to work toward loving yourself in this way, you will be able to accept not only the abundance that is here for you in this lifetime, but also the abundance that is waiting for you beyond it. This abundance is not merely of a physical nature. True abundance is about love. Loving yourself, Dear One, is about feeling how richly blessed you are in an abundant life, not just by what you have, but by who you are and by the love for yourself that lives in your heart.

Marinating in the Past

Dear One,

Even before you and I begin creating this letter, I can tell that you are feeling emotional. You are feeling sadness, joy, and love all wrapped up together. I see your mind flitting in many different directions, since this is such an extensive subject and one you have explored for years. It feels overwhelming because not only are you unsure of where to begin, you are also not certain you want to begin. Yet, you know how important this letter is. So if you can step aside for a moment, Dear One, and let Me come through, I will show you the way.

"Once upon a time," there was a little girl who was a very spiritual and sensitive child. She felt sorry when an ant got stepped on. She was sad when people were mean to each other, and she was confused when she couldn't understand the people she loved most. She just wanted everyone to be happy, but she could not make it so. She had no understanding of how life really worked. After all, she was just a little girl. She thought that if she was really lovable, things would change. But they didn't. Thus, she became very sad and did what many children do. She made up the belief that she wasn't good enough. Then she crawled up inside herself and began to live in her own little world.

One day, when no one was watching, she wandered into the woods. At first it felt wonderful. She could hug the trees and talk to the animals. But as darkness came on, the forest turned dense and gloomy, and she began to panic. The wonderful trees she loved so much began to look like ogres in the night. Day after day, night after night, the little girl waited for someone to come looking for her. Yet no one did.

Then one day a beautiful young woman came upon her and said, "Hello. I've been looking all over for you. Will you come with me?"

At first, the girl hesitated. "I don't know. I'm not supposed to talk to strangers."

The woman chuckled. "Oh, we're not strangers, little one. I actually know you quite well. Can't you see the resemblance between us?"

The girl stepped back, squinted, and said, "A little."

"Besides," said the young woman, "don't you want to be rescued?"

"Oh yes," the girl replied. So she took the woman's hand and was led out of the woods. As they walked, the young woman explained that the little girl would not be returning to her former home. Instead, from then on they would live together in a nice new home, and she would be the girl's new caretaker.

Within months, the little girl began to grow and blossom. She felt more loved and cared for than ever before. Yet, she was drawn to the forest, which held something familiar she missed without knowing why. So one day when no one was looking, she left her nice new home and wandered back into the woods. Once again, the trees turned into ogres in the night, and she felt afraid and sad. If only someone would come and rescue her.

Eventually, the beautiful woman came back, this time not as young as before. "Hello," she said. "I see you've found your way back into the scary woods. Why don't you come with me? Where we live is a much nicer place than this. Remember?"

The little girl thought about it and did remember how nice it was to be cared for and protected, so she took the woman's hand once again, and out of the woods they went. As time passed, the girl found herself going back into the forest time after time without explanation. She returned so often at intervals in her life that the woods themselves eventually felt familiar – not good, but somehow right. Each time she was rescued she noticed her caretaker becoming older and older, while she herself remained a child. This didn't bother her, however, because she knew the woman truly cared about her and would always be there to find her.

One day, when she had wandered into the woods again and was waiting to be rescued, the little girl saw a beautiful, shining light in the distance moving steadily toward her. As it approached, she saw that it was actually an exquisite child dressed in white, smiling with such radiance that she felt immediately comfortable and peaceful. A glance at this divine-looking creature revealed that she and this magical, evolved child were exact replicas of each other.

"Hello. It's time you came with me," the angelic child said.

"Who are you?" said the little girl.

"I am you," the child responded, "if you will but stay out of the woods."

"But this is where I live sometimes," said the girl adamantly, "and if I'm not here, who will notice that I am gone?"

The child replied, "I am here to rescue you, little one, and together we will be joyous, playful and safe. But you will have to trust me if you want to be rescued once and for all. Listen carefully. Take a deep breath, take my hand, and step into my light. All will be well – you will see."

"Will this hurt?" the little girl asked.

"Not one bit," replied the child, "I promise."

And so the little girl took a deep breath, grabbed the child's hand tightly, closed her eyes, and stepped into the glowing aura. Instantly, she was transformed into the beautiful evolved child, dressed in white. They were now one. She no longer felt sad or fearful. Instead, she felt lovable and worthy. She even felt a little grown up, although she remained young.

When she opened her eyes, the woman who had rescued her many times before, now much older, appeared before her. The woman smiled a loving smile, took the girl by the hand, and said, "We're going home." Together they walked out of the forest for good. The little girl never went back to the woods. Once in a while she would feel an inclination to do so, but she never did. She was happy, safe, and loved. And by the way, they are still living happily ever after.

You see, Dear One, this is the new story of you. This is the story you need to continue to tell yourself. You can still wander into the old one, but that's okay – you no longer live in the woods. You have discovered your joyous, playful, creative child within and have given yourself a happy childhood after all.

What a difference it would make in the world if people were to understand that there is a living, psychic being called "the inner child" that exists within everyone. Just as you are mind, body, and soul, you are also soul, adult, and child. The soul of you gives strength to the adult part of you, who in turn, is then able to take care of the child. It can be a wonderful parenting experience if you allow it. However, if you are unaware that this little one lives within, without knowing it, there will always be the inclination in the present life to relive the same old feelings and core beliefs of your "inner child." In other words, you will not be aware of how "little you" can easily rule "big you," causing havoc personally and in relationships with others. But if you pay attention to your reactions in life and take a moment to contemplate whether those reactions feel grown up or "little," there will be much more understanding within the self and in the world.

The key to loving yourself, Dear One, is loving all of you. This includes your own "little girl." For if you kept her in the woods, despite your being happy in other areas of life, you would soon discover that your happiness is short-lived. There would always be some feelings that reoccur and get in the way of your happiness and your ability to love you. In order for love of self to find its way into your life, you must acknowledge and love not only the happy parts of you, but the wounded parts as well. You must rescue the "little girl," so she can come home.

I tell you this story, Dear One, because it is perhaps the most important lesson about the past. The past is a good place to visit, but you wouldn't want to live there. Remembering your past is an invaluable tool for understanding yourself on a deeper level. Yet, if you live in the woods for too long, if you tie yourself emotionally to the past, you cannot move forward in the present. This doesn't mean you don't have memories of the past. It means you need to diffuse the power you have given these memories and no longer use them as an excuse to remain in the woods.

As your new story tells you, the evolved child can emerge from the wounded child. The wounded child says, "The past should have been different." The evolved child says, "How wonderful I've come so far and I don't have to worry anymore. I can have fun and be loved. I have someone to take care of me. I can be happy and fly." This transformation happens with a conscious decision on your part. You either stay and marinate in your old feelings, or you work through them and let them go.

You see, Dear One, if you take a hard-boiled egg, no matter how beautiful you paint it and how lovely it looks, if you seal it in a jar to marinate for years, it's going to come out stinky. If you stay mired in the past, no matter how familiar it is, it will not serve you well. What is important is to look at the past with the eyes of the adult you have become instead of with the eyes of the child you once were.

Then you can convert the energy of disappointment into the energy of accomplishment. You must always remember that you have the ability to do this because you are the Creator of your life.

Know that it is never too late to give yourself what you didn't have in childhood. If you needed someone to understand you, start understanding yourself. If you needed someone to accept you, start accepting yourself. If you needed love, find ways to love yourself. Give to the "little one" inside of you what she needs now. Be there for her the way you always wanted others to be there for you. Give her the words you always wanted to hear. You know what they are. Be the parent you always wanted to have.

I want you to know that the wondrous, beautiful child within has shown you what must be healed in order for you to see more of your own spiritual Light. She has given you the incredible opportunity to find more love for yourself. As much as you have rescued her from the woods, she in turn has shown you the way home. Continue to love her, for now she is part of your joy, rather than your pain.

Do you know, Dear One, that you were born a beautiful, spiritual child? Do you know that you still feel sorry when an ant gets stepped on? Do you know that you still cock your head when you listen? Do you know that you still make up sweet little melodies and sing them aloud? Do you know that you still can talk to the animals? Do you know how much you are loved?

You have never, nor will you ever, lose the essence of the sweet child you still are, because you are fanning that ember to a greater and greater flame. It is a beautiful thing to behold. Love the past for what it has given you. Bless it for the awakening of realizations that have led you to this point in time. Embrace yourself in the present moment, feeling the joy of the child within who is always ready to have fun, be happy, and love without question. For it is she who urges you to play. It is she who encourages you to create, and it is her undying love for you that permits you to continue to love as deeply

161

as you do. Both the wounded and the evolved child have helped lead you to Me. This is the divine birthright you have earned and found. Rejoice in it, Dear One, for this is who you were meant to be.

The Secret to Releasing Judgment

Dear One,

If there is such a thing as "the root of all evil," it certainly isn't money. It is judgment. Judgment always creates separation, and separation creates suffering. Judgment says, "I am right, you are wrong. I am good. You are bad. I am superior to you, or I am inferior to you." One of the prevailing judgments that has caused chaos and anguish in your world over centuries is, "My God is better than your God." Whether referring to countries, races, or individual personalities, judgment is any thought, feeling, or action that says, "You and I are not One." The most devastating judgment of all is against the self, because this is where judgment begins. If individuals would stop judging themselves, they would stop judging others. If the judgment of others would cease, there would be no need for countries to war with each other. If there would be no war, peace could prevail and your world could start anew. The power of judgment and how it is manifested is a determining factor of your world's condition, and it all starts with you, Dear One.

Most people believe that they cannot make a difference in the world because they are only one person. This is absolutely false. You can make a difference in your world right now by ending, or at the very least diminishing, the berating of yourself. This means you must attempt to eliminate negative self-talk, emotional spankings, and verbal punishments. Every human being battles with this. The only value judgment has is that it gives you the opportunity not to choose it when it slips into your head.

Your Society has certainly played a major part in the role of judgment. It has taught you that being hard on yourself is a good thing. The misconception is that if you are not hard on yourself, you won't be able to keep yourself "in line." Who knows what you would get away with if you weren't hard on yourself? Thus, judgment gets equated with having a good conscience, when they are actually two different things. I am here to tell you, Dear One, that being hard on yourself does not make you a better person. It does not build character or keep you from "crime." There is nothing positive about knocking yourself down – ever. The truth is that you can still maintain a very good conscience without succumbing to judgment.

Every time you reprimand yourself, you are choosing judgment. Every time you say you "should" or "shouldn't" think or feel something, you are judging yourself. Contrary to popular belief, there are no right or wrong feelings, or good or bad thoughts. Every feeling and thought has value because it tells you something about yourself. As I have said before, thoughts and feelings are your teachers. Therefore, if you put yourself down for having a feeling that you think you shouldn't have, not only will you make yourself feel badly about being who you are, but you will also miss out on the opportunity to learn more about yourself.

The cycle of judgment is a vicious one. When you judge yourself, you literally put yourself on trial and become the judge, jury, and executioner. As the jury, you pronounce yourself guilty of something you either thought, felt, said, or did. As the judge, you will have to designate a punishment for that crime, and believe me, you will every time. The executioner in you now has the honor of carrying out the sentence. Without exception, that sentence will withhold your happiness in some way, because you cannot feel guilty and happy at the same time. Therefore, in order to relieve your guilt, you must find a way to take away your happiness for the duration of your sentence, because you believe that you do not deserve happiness until you have paid for your crime. This kind of thinking is so instantaneous that you usually will have no awareness of what or when this is happening. Once you proclaim that you are guilty, you then must serve a self-imposed prison sentence of unhappiness. Some people give themselves short sentences and move on. Others choose sentences that last for weeks. Yet others give themselves life sentences for small offenses based on the biggest judgments.

It is important to know, Dear One, that when I speak of releasing judgment, I am not talking about taking away your opinions. There is a big difference between the two. When you judge, you scold. When you have an opinion, there is no admonishment. An opinion would sound like, "I don't know why I said that. I need to take a closer look at what was going on inside me that made me say something I didn't mean. That was definitely a mistake on my part. It's okay. I'm allowed to make mistakes, and I certainly do from time to time." A judgment sounds like, "I can't believe you're such an idiot to say such a thing. You shouldn't have said that. What were you thinking? What's wrong with you? You should know better."

The same process applies when you are observing another in a judgmental way. Expressing an opinion would sound like, "I don't like what she is doing. It would not be *my* choice to act that way, but everyone is different and has their own reasons for doing what they do." A judgment sounds like, "Who does she think she is, acting like that? She shouldn't be that way. She's such a _____."
I want you to know, Dear One, that everyone has the God-given "right of discernment" which is the right not to like something about someone else, or even yourself. However, when you judge yourself or another, you are choosing to feel superior, and this creates separateness rather than Oneness. Since every judgment you make about

yourself or another creates negative karma, one of the best ways to evolve is to make fewer judgments and have more opinions.

For this to happen, you must free yourself from your own suffering by releasing the punitive thoughts you have about yourself and replacing them with understanding. There is always a reason why you think, feel, and act the way you do. Nothing is coincidental in that way. When you find that you are condemning yourself, stop and take the time to understand what is going on within you that makes you feel worse about yourself. Use acceptance and understanding as your tools, not a gavel. It's okay to feel badly if you are experiencing remorse for having hurt someone, for example. But know that you can feel contrite without going to the dark place where judgment lives.

The secret to releasing judgment from your life is actually quite simple and pleasant. Instead of becoming your own judge, jury and executioner, become an awesome detective. In other words, replace your judgmental thoughts with investigative ones. Find yourself curious instead of guilty. Once you are interested about why you thought, felt, or acted in a certain way, judgment will lessen. Become more invested in being curious than in putting yourself down. Change your verbal repertoire from "What's wrong with you?" to "Hmm. That's interesting." Use the words, "I wonder." "I wonder why I'm feeling this way. I wonder why I needed to say that. I wonder why I'm thinking negative thoughts. I wonder why that person is acting that way toward another."

You see, Dear One, when you are curious enough to wonder about yourself or someone else, rather than giving in to the punitive tactic, you are on your way to evolving as a soul. The wonderful thing about employing curiosity as a way to curtail judgment is that, when you become curious about yourself, it indicates a willingness on your part to have an idea about yourself other than a negative one. It gives you the opportunity to turn the feeling of darkness within into a feeling of light. When you open yourself to becoming more curious about yourself, you will find that the answers you are looking for as to why you think, say, or do things will come much more quickly, because you are no longer punitive. Rather, you are receptive. In the moment of releasing judgment, Dear One, you will have transformed yourself from a judge into a curious and benign sleuth.

Whenever you find that you are beating yourself up, stop and look at yourself and the situation with curiosity. Investigate. Talk to yourself about it, forgive yourself, and get back on track with yourself. Every moment spent in the negative ego is precious time lost from remembering who you really are. So when you choose judgment, you take away from what you really want most in life, which is to be loved and accepted.

I tell you this, Dear One, because, with the exception of learning from it, no good will ever come from judgment. The understanding you are looking for will come when you befriend curiosity. If you can do this, you will no longer be your own worst enemy. Instead, you will be your own best friend.

Letting go of judgment is one of the major keys to growing as a human and evolving as a soul. When judgment is suspended, it is so much easier to be with yourself. You no longer have to worry about what you see inside yourself, because you no longer judge what you see. When you no longer judge what you see, you are no longer afraid of yourself. You are then able to realistically assess that you are not perfect, and that there will be times when your human side gets the better of you. This is okay. When this happens, you must remind yourself that you are a work in progress, and that continuing the journey of discovery of what is right with you is far more powerful than obsessing about what is wrong with you.

Do you remember the time on the beach when without warning a huge bumblebee buzzed so close to you that you jumped out of your chair like the lift-off at Cape Canaveral? You swung at it so hard with your book that the dust jacket flew off and sailed halfway down the beach. Off you ran to retrieve it, stumbling along the way, with that pesky little bee hot on your heels. When you finally found your way back to your chair, quite humbled by the scene of it all, there waiting for you was the bumblebee, ready for round two. This time, instead of running away, you were angry. You rose from your chair ready to do battle. If this thing was out to get you and you couldn't live in peace with each other, it was going to be all-out war! And with that in mind, the pesky little critter buzzed his little wings and left.

This episode in your life, Dear One, symbolizes the attacks and the unnecessary "stinging" of the self. By running away and not facing how you hurt yourself emotionally, you will always stumble and fall. It is only when you are ready to fight judgment that you can begin to love yourself.

When you stop verbally and emotionally stinging yourself, you will feel relief, compassion, and a love for you that you have never felt before. As I stated in the previous letter, it is then that you will begin to associate such love with the Higher Love that has always been there with you and for you. This is the prize of life, Dear One. The reward you get from releasing judgment is knowing and feeling your own soul. Liberating yourself from judgment will always lead you to Me. It will also free you from judging others, so that you can understand them, despite what they do. This is the answer, not only to your own prayers, but also to the prayers of your world. Every day millions of people pray for peace. They can have this peace if they will find it within themselves. And this can only happen when they stop the war within.

Know that your inner work is paying off for yourself and in the world. Every time you change judgment into curiosity, you alter the world in a positive way. Every time you make the choice to love yourself or another, you have added love to the Universal

Consciousness. That love returns to you, filling you with even more love, which in turn expands the love within you and in your world. Before you know it, you will end up truly believing and experiencing that love is really all there is, and the rest of life is just there to help you find it. When you finally feel this with all your heart and soul, Dear One, it is then we get our wings.

Growth Is Learning To Be a Disappointment

Dear One,

You might think it odd that one's soul would invite its human counterpart to engage in being a disappointment. From My point of view, this request is an important ingredient for learning to love oneself. According to your world, to be a disappointment is nothing short of failure. How many times have you heard it said that disappointing a loved one has been a weight someone has carried around for years? Yet, disappointment is an essential part of life – no one escapes life without disappointment. The people you love the most will disappoint you the most because you love them so much. And the people who love you the most will be disappointed by you for the very same reason. There is no getting around the fact that the world and the people in it can be very disappointing. Despite Society's view that being a disappointment is a major character flaw, you might consider these two questions: Are you aware that the major disappointments in your life have propelled you to find yourself? And have you ever considered that someone else's growth may also be a direct result of you disappointing them?

Disappointment is not only a fact of life; it is also a necessary component for attaining self-love. This is because you cannot be everything to everyone, nor can they be everything to you. You are not a super human nor were you meant to be. Loving yourself requires that, most of the time, your first concern has to be *you*. There will be times when you will have to learn to tolerate disappointing yourself and others. This does not mean that you should look forward to or purposely try to be a disappointment. It simply means that you matter. You count. What you think and feel is as important as anyone else's thoughts and feelings. And if you must risk disappointing others in order to be yourself, then so be it. You can only be who you are, and they can only be who they are.

When you are willing to be a disappointment, you are willing to be loyal to yourself. Society embraces the concept of loyalty when it comes to another, yet those loyal to themselves are often viewed as self-centered and self-indulgent. Consequently, you have grown up with an ingrained belief that others are supposed to be more important than you are. Dear One, hear Me when I say that this is not the best way to love someone. The greatest gift you can give another is your own love of self. When you are able to fill up your own emotional well with love for yourself, it will naturally spill over to everyone else. You will have much more love, generosity, and abundance to give to others because you will have given it first to yourself. You will hear Me say this many times throughout this book. And if you care for everyone else's needs instead of your own, not only will you deplete yourself, but you will also ultimately betray yourself. To consistently lay yourself down for another will never serve either of you well. You will not live your life joyously because you will have lost the true essence of who you are.

When you allow yourself to be a disappointment in a positive way, you will become comfortable with saying "no" for the benefit of all concerned. Disappointing others will mean facing the fear of not being liked, which is quite prevalent in your world. Once again, I agree that it is wonderful to be liked. But if you are unwilling to risk losing others for fear that they will no longer like you or may leave you, then you are compromising yourself and taking the enormous risk of losing *you*.

Consequently, the dilemma of to be or not to be a disappointment comes down to one very important question: how will you know when it is right to choose what you want over what another wants? The answer, Dear One, is this: when you are giving to others, you need to be aware of whether you are giving to them out of love or out of fear. If you feel no resentment at surrendering your own wishes, you will know it is love. In fact, it will make you happy to see them happy. The expansive feeling you gain from being able to give in this way is what love of self is all about. When you give to another out of fear, however, the results are quite different. Even though you made the choice, you will feel a constriction of silent resentment and anger within. You may not feel this right away, but it will be there. When you are unwilling to disappoint another – be it a friend, a partner, or a child – you will automatically create a subtle distance between the two of you. And the relationship is bound to suffer.

The key to tolerating being a disappointment is to learn to tolerate disappointing yourself. Everyone disappoints himself or herself. What matters most is how you react to being a disappointment. Do you berate, condemn, and judge yourself? Or do you try to understand the inner workings that caused you to be who you didn't want to be at that particular moment? Your answers to these questions will also determine how you respond to others when they disappoint you.

One of the best truths you can hold onto in life is knowing that you are a spiritual being first and a human being second. To find your way into that spiritual space, you must be willing to acknowledge and allow all of your humanness. Therefore, you must understand that you can be the most spiritual person in the world and still be a disappointment. This is permissible, as well as necessary, for your spiritual and emotional wellbeing. It is wonderful when you can finally agree with others that, yes indeed, you certainly can be a disappointment. You can also tell them that this probably won't be the last time you will disappoint them, either. This attitude will take you into the far reaches of self-love, Dear One, because it shows that you are still willing to love yourself despite your imperfections.

Finally, I want to say this to you: You are not here to live up to the expectations of others. Yours are high enough. You also did not come to this Earth to put others before you. You came here to experience equal importance. If you want to understand disappointment on a more spiritual level, you must realize that when others are disappointed in you, it is their preconceived idea of you that fails them, not you. And when you are disappointed in others, the failing is simply because of your preconceived notion of who they are or who you think they should be. So accept those feelings of disappointment with the realization that you optimistically expected them to be different than who they really were in that moment. In this way, you continue to understand that others are not here to live up to your expectations, either.

Know, Dear One, that you can never disappoint Me. As I watch you move closer to remembering who you are, I am filled with love for you. And if you had not followed this path and grown as you have, I would still be filled with the same love for you. A soul's love for its human personality is unconditional. In your willingness to accept your humanness and your ability to disappoint another without judging yourself, you have taken another step in your growth as a human and in My evolution as a soul. This lesson has helped you find courage, compassion, conviction, and the capacity for love. And as always, everything you discover about yourself leads you to Me.

173

Don't Let Anyone Treat You Less Than You Treat Yourself

Dear One,

There are many significant words which, when lived, will lead you to finding love of self. Compassion, non-judgment, courage, acceptance, and honesty are just a few. The word I am thinking of for this particular letter, however, is not one that most would believe is notable. Yet, if you were to incorporate this word into your repertoire, not only would you find it empowering, but you would also discover it to be a vehicle for changing your life. This marvelous word is "unacceptable." Truly experiencing this word will set you on the path to self-respect and, ultimately, self-love.

One of the most powerful efforts you can make toward attaining self-love is to look at how you treat yourself physically, emotionally, and spiritually. If you are judgmental, unforgiving, or do not believe that you are good enough, you will attract those who feel the same way about themselves and thereby will treat you accordingly. When this happens, because you tolerate doing it to yourself, you will feel compelled to tolerate unacceptable behavior and emotional putdowns from others; thus, you will allow them to treat you with less consideration than you deserve. Until you are willing to treat yourself with kindness and respect, you will continue to receive unacceptable treatment from others.

In your early adult life, it was easy to give away your "power," your sense of self. You thought you were supposed to. Fairy tales, soap operas, and love songs taught you that making someone else "the one" was how you were supposed to love. They emphasized the notions that you could not live without another, you must avoid rejection at all costs, and "you're nobody 'til somebody loves you." You learned that, in order to avoid losing them, whoever you were in a relationship with must be more important than you are. Therefore, whenever you placed another above you, the only place left for you was below. It was then you also learned that the price to pay for losing yourself in any relationship is far too high. The ideas you were taught about being in a relationship were wonderful for romance novels, but certainly did not work in real life.

There is no doubt that relationships are the most potent and compelling experiences you can have in life. They are paramount to understanding and loving yourself, because they always give you the opportunity to learn more about yourself and others. They are one of the truest tests of whether you will retain your powerful sense of self while sharing it with another, or whether you will simply give it away.

When you treat yourself with respect and do not allow another to treat you with less than this, you definitely take the risk of being rejected. You also may have to be the one to do the rejecting and walk away from someone who does not treat you well if you love yourself enough. It can be painful to choose yourself over the one you love when there is little hope that he or she will meet your need for respect. Therefore, you must be the ultimate authority on how you are being treated, for no one, Dear One, can put you down without your permission. The better you treat yourself, the more you will require others to treat you the same. When you are able to set this boundary for yourself, you will move swiftly in the direction of loving yourself.

Some may wonder how karmic relationships fit into the concept of unacceptable treatment by another. I must say that no relationship is meant to be lived in misery and suffering. If you choose to stay in such a one, it is not necessarily karmic. It is your choice according to your free will. Karma can be the excuse given in order to stay in a relationship because certain pre-arrangements between souls may include some sort of dissension. This does not mean, however, that they have come here to live an entire lifetime together in discontent. No soul comes here to live a life of unhappiness. More often than not, souls come into this lifetime to learn what is needed to be able to move on to the next stage of their lives and erase the karma between them. Even soul mates can come together during a lifetime to learn and grow and can eventually leave each other for the good of all involved. This is why, Dear One, no matter the relationship, if you feel treated less than the standard you have set for yourself, then an act of love would be to leave that relationship – not only for you, but also for the other.

Loving the self is not an easy task. It requires a fearless spirit and challenges you to become your own hero in the adventure of life. Always remember that how well you treat yourself will determine the quality of your life. When you treat yourself with the utmost of dignity, you will no longer be afraid of losing another, because you will have the most steadfast friend by your side at all times. You will have *you*.

Feeling Humble and Magnificent in the Same Breath

Dear One,

Many believe that to feel humble and magnificent at the same time is impossible. From My perspective, however, when you begin remembering who you are, it is not only possible, but also probable. In your world, the idea of being humble can conjure up various mental pictures. One may be of a person with head lowered, eyes cast downward, and possibly even subservient to someone or something. In the eyes of some people, this image might be enveloped in a mystical haze of goodness and spirituality. Another scenario might indicate that to be humble one must feel unworthy or undeserving. From this interpretation comes the sense that to be a good person, one should feel deficient and perhaps even belittle oneself to some degree, suppressing any expression of pride. In fact, if in your world you are observed as being a humble person, you are often seen as a nicer person, and sometimes even a better one – whether this is true or not. Many people also believe that humility is a requirement of religion. By feeling unworthy to be in the presence of God, they believe they are living according to God's wishes.

These concepts of humility imply that lowering yourself will raise you up in the eyes of others. I am here to tell you that this kind of humility is not everything it's cracked up to be. Although I am not one to dismiss another's religious beliefs, I must reiterate that it is impossible for you to be unworthy. Everyone is and always will be worthy, because God lives within each and every one of you. I continue to address this issue because it is time for your world to realize that no one is here to be less than another. None of you have come here to diminish who you are. You have come into this lifetime to realize your Light and express it in an uplifting, glorious manner. Therefore, you need not bow your head so as to feel small before God. Instead, bow your head out of love and reverence for the One who created you from His Love.

There is another way of feeling humble without making yourself inconsequential. I will make my point by once again reminding you of who you really are. You are an incredible Divine vibration of energy that has come to this Earth for a time in which to experience the physical life that will continue your evolution as a soul. You have been given eternity in which to experience the Creator's world in any way you choose. You have the opportunity to experience different and exciting lifetimes throughout your existence. You have been given free will so that you may grow at your own pace and in your own timeframe. You have been given the miracle of seeing firsthand how your God-given creation constitutes every manifestation in your life. During your visit here you are never left alone. You have been endowed with Divine beings that are always at your side to help guide you through this life on Earth. You can never be destroyed, because you have been created as Eternal Life. Therefore, anyone you have loved will always remain within your existence. You never lose them. Lastly, since God is ever present within you, you have the ability to handle anything that comes your way.

I repeat these words to you, Dear One, because humility is tantamount to the joy and wonder that comes from such realizations. You are a magnificent soul who has been given an extraordinary opportunity to express your uniqueness in this Universe for all eternity. When you can feel this in your heart, you cannot help but feel awed by it. This kind of awe, the kind that takes your breath away, represents the true essence of humility. In the gratefulness and miracle of it all, you are humbled.

The awareness of this understanding is how you "inherit the Earth," Dear One. If you replace the words "humble" or "meek" with the word "awe," you will see what I mean. You will inherit the Earth when you embrace the legacy of who you are in this Earthly experience and when you know that you really are "in this world, but not of it." You will inherit the Earth when you recognize that you and the Creator are One. Then the miracle that is the Earth will become yours to experience. To feel this in your heart and soul will be humbling and magnificent at the same time.

Speaking of magnificence – when you were a child, you remembered your brilliance. All children do. If you watch them, you will see how they rejoice in their mud pies, crayon drawings, and all their other works of creation. They have no problem announcing to the world, "Look how good I am! Aren't I wonderful? I made this!" The only way they remain small is in their stature. As youngsters, they may have "little" abilities, but they are not merely little human beings. They are joyous souls reveling in the magnificence of who they really are, because they inherently remember that they are powerful Creators, even if it is a simple mud pie.

When children learn that announcing their magnificence to the world is no longer considered appropriate and acceptable, most children stop feeling this sense of exaltation. No boasting allowed! There is also an age-old scolding in your Society called, "Who do you think you are?" Many a Light in your world has been extinguished because of that phrase. With that admonishment comes the belief that thinking well of oneself and expressing it to others does not earn the Good Housekeeping Seal of Approval. When I urge you to feel your magnificence, it is not about succumbing to arrogant pride based on your insecurities. This kind of pomposity gives the word "proud" a bad name, as evidenced by the church sign you passed the other day which read, "If you're singing your own praises, you're in the wrong key."

In order to incorporate love of self into your life, Dear One, you must give yourself permission to speak of yourself with high regard. It is important to feel proud of who you are. I encourage you to accept compliments and give them out freely as well. Being able to speak of yourself lovingly does not take something away from anyone else. Everyone has their own Light. Always remember that letting your Light shine does not lessen the Light of another. Yours is stunningly beautiful, so do not suppress its radiance.

Allow yourself to sing the praises of whatever is true about you. You do not have to announce it to the world like a child with mud pies, but if you do, it is not a sin. In fact, it just may give another person permission to do the same. I advocate looking for what is right in yourself and feeling good about it. If you cannot find pleasure and joy in *you*, how can you find this in another? In this lifetime, I am constantly reminded that human beings have forgotten to be amazed at themselves. So, Dear One, rejoice in your magnificence and Divinity. You are all the Light of the world. No soul is more magnificent than another. If every human being would believe this, no harm would ever come to another.

Each human being has the capacity to feel magnificent and humble in the same breath. Together, these two qualities can summon up the remembrance of the inspirational awe and exaltation of life. If you ever hear yourself saying, "Who do you think you are?" reply with this: "I will tell you who I am. I am a Divine Child of God with Divine rights of my own. I am One with the Source of all Creation. I am an Infinite being with Infinite possibilities. I am the Creator of my life. I am eternal. I am kindness and wisdom. I am unconditional love. I am utterly magnificent. That is who I am." Never has a truer statement been made about you or anyone. If you have a hard time believing it, then this is where your work lies.

Years ago, as you were floating on your raft on the lake with your friend, you looked up at your newly built house and joyfully flung open your arms. With complete abandon you declared, "I am magnificent." In that moment you experienced the unmitigated awe of *you* as a Creator. This was you at your best, Dear One, because you were feeling the ecstasy of who you really are. When throughout your life you can throw up your arms and shout the divine exaltation "I am Magnificent," many hearts in the Universe, not just your own, will soar. For in these moments you will announce yourself as the brilliant Light you are and feel the humble splendor of it all.

When You Trust in You, You Trust in the Very Wisdom That Created You

Dear One,

All roads do not lead to Rome. All roads lead to trust. This is why I have saved this particular letter for the last in this juncture of our journey. Everything I have said to you thus far about life, love, and God has led to your learning to trust yourself. Trust begins with the desire to know yourself on more than just a superficial level. Becoming more aware of your thoughts and feelings and taking responsibility for them will lead you steadily down the path of trust. Letting go of the past so that it no longer rules you is essential to trusting yourself. Reducing fear, releasing judgment, and treating yourself with respect are all areas of inner work that will propel you forward to gaining trust. Knowing that you are not alone because you are divinely guided not only by Me, but also by others in the Universe who love you, adds to your assurance of trust. And when you trust yourself, you will know that you do not have to have all the answers to life, and it is all right. When you add love of self to this equation, you have acquired the icing on the cake. Trust is one of the highest forms of love. And like every other accomplishment in your life, trust must be earned. Therefore, you will have to earn your own trust. With your efforts to know and love yourself described in the previous letters, trust will lovingly arrive on your doorstep.

When you can genuinely depend on who you are, you will truly believe in what you say you believe, and will act accordingly. You will be able to trust in your ability to cope. You will accept that every resource you will ever need to get through any situation in life will be provided for you when you need it. You will trust yourself enough to know that you will not make the same mistakes over and over again. You will make the best decisions you can, and if you don't, you will trust that you will love yourself enough to move on without judgment. Now do you see why all roads lead to trust?

It is easy to trust yourself when life seems to be going your way and there are no so-called glitches to contend with. It is wonderful when life flows smoothly and all is well. However, the truest test of trusting yourself will be when fear enters your life. Can you still trust that all is well when life isn't the way you want it to be, or the way you think it should be? Do you allow doubt and worry to overtake your trust, or do you let trust reign supreme? During times of struggle, do you remember your Light and know that help is on the way? Can you trust that what you ask for will come to you even if it doesn't appear to come when you want it most? Can you trust that your prayers will be answered even though the answer may not arrive in the package you had expected? Or do you lose trust and question your beliefs all over again?

This is why trust is one of the highest forms of loving yourself, Dear One. It is not something that is given to you. You must earn it by working on knowing yourself. The more you know yourself, the more trust you earn. Trust challenges you to believe in the process of life that will take you where you are meant to be at the right and proper time. In other words, if you plant tomato seeds in your garden and then spend the next few days digging them up to see if they have sprouted, they never will. You must trust that those seeds will grow into beautiful tomatoes meant to nourish you, and that this will happen in its right time.

You see, Dear One, trust requires a certain amount of surrender. Letting go of what you see with your Earthly eyes and trusting that your spiritual eyes will see the bigger picture is not always easy.

However, when you can get to that place, you will move toward the highest level of trust, which is faith. Faith is the ultimate acceptance of trust. When you have faith, you are willing to let go of what you know intellectually and trust something beyond yourself. When faith guides you, you can trust that what is going on in your life will take you to where you need to go on your ultimate path, even when stumbling blocks appear.

It takes this kind of faith to believe that, no matter what the circumstance, something is happening for the good of all involved, even though you cannot see it. I say this to you because many situations in life can make this seem untrue. For example, having lost a loved one, you may say, "This is not what is best for me." But how do you know this was not best for your loved one and his or her soul? And just because you're not feeling good about it, how do you know that the Divine isn't taking place for your best interest? Always bear in mind that you, like everyone else in this world, are a soul first and a human second. The soul's agenda will always take precedence over the human's agenda. When you trust deeply enough to know this, you will have discovered the essence of faith.

When you trust in the Divine process of life, Dear One, all things are possible. Continue to trust in the possibilities of life, not the probabilities, because the *possibilities* will always take you to a higher place. Live in the moment, but look over the horizon to the future, because trusting in the now will create a trusting future. Go forward with each day as if it were the greatest day of your life, because it is.

Trust in yourself as you do when driving your car. When you come to a curve in the road, you don't stop because you're not sure that the road is still there. You trust that it's going to be there. Do the same in life, Dear One. Trust that your path is still there, and if the path takes a detour to avoid something, it's all right because your trust in the path will ultimately take you where you want to go.

Earning your own trust is a sacred act of love. It is a joy surpassed by no other, for when you trust in yourself, you will feel safe in the world. Trust that whatever is going on in your life will take you where you need to go to find your ultimate path. Know that in every phase of your life a door will open to answer the needs of the moment. Let your faith acknowledge that you trust that the Creative Force of God has a plan and that you are a part of it. And since this Force resides within you, don't be afraid to be led by it. When you can trust in this, the highest of levels, you will trust in the very wisdom that created you. This is the epitome of trust. And it is this kind of trust, Dear One, that will lead you toward making this your last lifetime.

Section VI:

Open These Letters
When You Want to
Remember the Soul of You

Alone at Last

Dear One,

I can tell you without equivocation that you would not be where you are today without having spent countless hours alone. Over the years you have devoted a great deal of time to contemplating your life, writing down dreams, and journaling. What I am about to convey is based on observing you throughout your life and knowing you like no other. Although you may not be aware of this, some of your most joyous moments in life have been when you were alone. As a child, I watched you roll marbles on a plate for hours and listened to you teach your dolls how to read and write. I saw daydream after daydream propel your creativity to give birth to new ideas and manifestations. I watched you sitting on a beach staring at the waves and listening to the sound of God's Breath. For years I have joined you in the writing process, witnessing your intense need to know yourself deeply, and I have wallowed in joy when your heartfelt thoughts came alive on the page. It has been a pleasure watching you enjoy your own company during these times alone.

While searching for yourself, you found Me. Ultimately, you exchanged the intellectual approach to knowing yourself as a soul for *experiencing* yourself as a soul. This has come about, Dear One, because of your willingness to spend alone time with yourself, which has been life-changing for you. Consequently, you have discovered that you are more than you ever thought possible. From the little "marble roller" to the woman you have become, I have had the honor of being in the physical body of one who has used her free will to follow the path I have set forth. Granted, there have been detours along the way, but these are part of the wonderful package of being human and Divine. No path is ever totally straight. How much fun would that be?

I tell you this, Dear One, because all human beings, whether or not they remember it, long for a connection with who they really are. Knowing who you are as a soul does not have to be a mystery, nor was it ever meant to be. Connecting with your soul can be experienced in everyday life in a myriad of ways. Some people connect to their souls through music, dance or another art. Others connect by being of service. There are those who touch their souls through yoga, prayer, or meditation – or by trying to be the best person they can be. It doesn't matter how the connection is made. It doesn't even matter if one is aware of this connection or not, although such awareness can be quite exciting. Therefore, whether you are a dancer, a caregiver, a meditator, or simply striving to be your authentic self, alone time is a necessary ingredient for knowing yourself as a soul. The dancer and musician need alone time to practice. The caregiver needs alone time to recuperate and regain enough energy to give back. The meditator needs alone time to find the still, small voice within, and the one who seeks to know the self needs time alone for introspection.

For those who wish to know themselves as the magnificent souls they are, solitary time is essential. Many in your part of the world are not comfortable with this, because they are quite busy filling up time with "doing" activities, thus avoiding being alone with themselves. This creates a paradox that can control their lives. They claim that they want to "stop the world and get off," but they don't, because they fear what will happen if they do. If they do decide to get off, they will be faced with having more time alone with themselves, which is a frightening prospect for many. Yet, this is exactly what people must do if they want to find their soul and the inner peace they are looking for.

If human beings would be alone with themselves for fifteen minutes a day, it would make a significant difference in their lives. It doesn't matter if you are sitting in a chair and letting your mind wander to far-off places or driving and letting yourself drink in the Divine beauty of Nature along the way; nor does it matter whether you're taking a walk or just sitting on a rock. I encourage any kind of alone time, no matter what or where it happens. When you turn off the radio, television, or any other background noise and allow yourself to just "be," you will give yourself the opportunity to hear the sweet stillness of life and experience what you are feeling in that given moment.

It would be of great benefit to you, Dear One, if you would consider spending more time alone with yourself in Nature. When God created Nature, it was an act of love not only to provide for Man's physical survival, but for his emotional survival, as well. This is why your species loves and needs to be in Nature, and why many flock to the mountains, valleys, beaches, and forests as often as they can. Nature soothes and enables people to relax, to let go of gnawing thoughts and be replenished. Nature provides them with easy access to their souls and fulfills their longing to connect to their Divine roots. In Nature, you inherently feel you are in the presence of something greater than you are, yet you are also an integral part of it. When you tune in to the beauty of your surroundings, you can actually feel the pulse of the Almighty. And when you feel this pulse, you will recognize that the same heartbeat resides within you. The joy of this experience is what it is like to meet your soul. Nature is a place where you can actually feel the Presence of God in His utter splendor. It is here for your healing, rejuvenation, well-being and joy.

191

I want to tell you something about Nature, Dear One. Nature has buffered storms most people could not understand. It has seen drought, flood, and cataclysms, but has never stopped believing in its ability to exist and survive. The rotting tree does not see itself as dead, rather it sees itself as the fertilizer that will bring forth new trees from the seeds it dropped before it fell. Nature can teach you amazing lessons if you pay attention. Never underestimate its power. It has its own Divine vibrational energy that not only has the power to understand you, but to heal you as well.

Your love of Nature and your need to spend alone time outdoors is especially strong because of Me. When you are outside you sometimes feel this love coming through by osmosis. This is because I carry within Me many lifetimes as an American Indian. In fact, a multitude of your fellow human beings who have a strong affinity for Nature have led previous lives as the American Indian or through other cultures that value Nature. During My incarnations as an Indian, I was physically, emotionally, and spiritually connected to the wind, the trees, the deer, and the brook. I felt the presence of the Great Spirit around Me at all times. As a culture, we honored the sacredness of all things in Nature. It is why you have a special affinity for trees, and why you cry when you see them needlessly destroyed.

During many a walk, I have watched you go to a tree and place your arms around it without knowing why you had the impulse to do so. At such times, Dear One, you needed to feel closer to your own soul and to God. By embracing the tree, you were gathering the strength you needed to revitalize yourself. You used the power of Nature to raise your vibration. I nudged you to do this, for I know that when you are in Nature you are in touch with the vital force of the Universe, which in turn touches your own vital energy. I also know that Nature has the ability to love you back. So when you need to feel more loved, Dear One, I will always guide you toward a tree.

Being alone in Nature clearly provides an open gateway to sensing the presence of one's soul. Feelings of awe, joy and wonder are always heightened when you step outside your door to the outside world. Some of your most delicious, insightful moments in life have been when taking a walk or just sitting in your lawn chair listening to the crickets or the birds. Nature has the power to escalate the process of knowing Me because, when you are in it, you naturally halt the inner chatter of your mind and give yourself the opportunity to hear the God Voice of your soul.

I know I have said this many times, but I must repeat Myself. There is no one more important to get to know in this world than *you*. Therefore, any time you can spend alone with yourself will be immensely valuable. I especially enjoy sharing your solitude when you are in the car. I love hearing you talk to yourself out loud and I relish your sense of humor during these conversations. I also commend your willingness to connect with yourself, no matter what you are feeling and I celebrate how important this has become to you. And with utter jubilation, Dear One, I embrace your eagerness to talk to Me and listen for My reply.

If you were to have My ability to look back at your life in its totality, you would see that you have felt less alone in many of your solitary moments than you have at any other time in your life. These times spent with yourself have given you not only the ability to be alone, but also the wisdom that being alone is one of the most beautiful experiences of a lifetime.

This is why I will never cease to let you know when it is time for you to have some alone time. You will feel the urge and will know what it means. Whether you are in Nature or not, spending time alone with yourself will always help you refill your emotional well so that you may continue in the service you have asked for. Being alone will help you reconnect with what you want in life, and will have the power to heal whatever needs to be healed. Most of all, spending time alone with yourself will give us time to be together, just the two of us. Hence, you will remember that you are never alone and that life is a beautiful play for you to experience to the fullest. Don't forget to hug a tree once in a while, Dear One. If you can wrap your arms around the tree and be still for a few moments, you will feel the tree wrapping its arms around you and you will feel your connection to Me as the love of God flows through you.

Right Here, Right Now

Dear One,

Right now in your world, one of the most profound aspects of spirituality is the concept of "the present moment." It is no coincidence that this time-honored Buddhist perception is finding its way into the present-day psyche. Now is the right and perfect time for Mankind to comprehend what the present moment is all about. Although you can have memories of the past and resurrect them in the present, the past no longer exists. It is gone forever. The future only exists in your imagination until it finally arrives to become the present moment once again. Therefore, there is only right now. Being in the present moment is My natural state. It is where I live. Every soul relishes in the here and now because it knows there is nothing else. It is only the *human* mind that lives in the past and the future. To remember the present, Dear One, you must spend even the smallest amount of time paying attention to the delicious, intriguing, and exciting moments of now. Then you will have the opportunity to find the entry point for realizing your true identity as a soul.

Fifteen years ago, you first realized that you were able to hear My voice while you were on vacation. As you spent hours each day writing, your mind was not focused on yesterday or tomorrow. It was not invested in what you were going to eat for lunch or what you were going to do later. You didn't even know what time it was, nor did you care. During that time you were totally concentrated in the present moment. One day, sitting there in a peaceful stillness, writing whatever came to you, your mind suddenly began to fill up with loving thoughts. Your heart was flooded with so much love that you thought it would burst. You were so overwhelmed by this love that you gasped and began to cry without knowing why. As you feverishly continued to write down the words you were hearing, you knew that something miraculous was happening. You knew you were feeling the true essence of *you*. Never before had you felt such vastness. Not only was it a beautiful awakening for you, but it was also the first of many written communications between us. And it happened because you were totally in the present moment. By being alive in the here and now, you allowed yourself to notice Me showing up.

Many others who read this book will want to experience who they are as a soul. Becoming comfortable with being alone is one of the necessary preparations, which is why I addressed this experience in the last letter. You do not have to be alone in order to be in the present moment, but permitting yourself to be alone from time to time will help you tolerate *staying* in the present moment. To connect with your soul, you must become aware of what is happening here and now, since this is the only place you can find Me. One of the best ways to experience being in the moment is to become more aware of your five senses. We will save the sixth for another letter. Sight, sound, smell, touch and taste are the ingredients you will need to begin this practice. The exercise I am about to give you is best practiced when alone. However, the better at it you become, the more you will realize that you can be fully present at any moment in time, no matter what is going on around you, whether you are alone or not.

The other day, while sitting in your screened-in porch, the thought came to you to be in the present moment for five minutes. And you did just that. Very simply, you put your book down, took a deep breath, and became very still. Your only mission for those five minutes was to be the observer of what was going on around you, using your senses to experience what it felt like to be right here, right now. Let me remind you, Dear One, of what you experienced during that short period of time. At various intervals, you heard the calls of the cardinal, the morning dove, and the hawk. You noticed the sound of the air conditioner turning on and off. You watched leaves on the trees flutter in the breeze. You paid attention to the rhythm of your breath while looking at the different colors of the sky. You felt the heat of your coffee cup when you picked it up. Not only did you smell the coffee's aroma, but you also felt its warmth as it flowed down your throat. Your attention turned to cars heard in the distance. As you focused on the weight of your body sitting on the chair, you became aware of what your glasses felt like sitting on your nose. Then you noticed the ringing in your ears. As you watched a squirrel run by, you also saw a little yellow butterfly zigzag through the air, and you were amazed at how fast it could fly and change direction. You heard your parrot talking to herself in the house, and as your dog jumped onto your lap for a quick hello, you felt the softness of his coat. You noticed how coarse the arm of your wicker chair felt with its rivers of grooves. You reveled at the crescendo and decrescendo of the grasshoppers' song. As you listened to the buzz of a passing fly, you spied a lone white flower on the magnolia bush in front of you. An airplane overhead claimed your attention for a while, as did the varying colors of the grass and adjoining bushes. As a cloud floated by, you noticed how still your dog was as he lay beside your chair, basking in his own present moment. You examined the design of the fabric of your robe and the freckles on your legs. Finally, you felt the smoothness of the pen in your hand, and you came back to the rhythm of your breath once again.

At last, you witnessed in wonderment how magnificent life was in those five minutes when you felt nothing but peace, calm, and stillness. You were not being held hostage by thoughts of what happened yesterday or what you needed to do later on. Instead of thinking, you just allowed yourself to be. You were feeling the power of life itself and the power of you in it. During those five minutes, nothing else mattered. It was just you and Me observing life in the present moment.

If everyone would practice this five minute exercise once a day, anywhere, not only would they feel a difference in their emotional state, they would also give themselves the opportunity to open the portal to their soul. On this particular day, you chose to be on the porch. Later, you also discovered that being present in the shower can be quite marvelous. When you pay attention to how soothing the water is, how your body feels when the water hits your head, and how sweet the soap smells, taking a shower is no longer an ordinary experience. It is a joy. The same can happen when you drive. Feel your hands on the wheel and drink in the scenery along the way. I guarantee you will see things you haven't ever noticed before, although they have always been there. Know that these five minutes are your gifts to yourself and your soul. The more you practice being present, Dear One, the more opportunity you will have to experience who you are as a soul. And when you give yourself the occasion to listen to your own loving, soulful thoughts, you will feel the immense peace and joy that comes with being in the present moment.

One of the best ways to remind yourself to be in the present moment throughout the day is to ask yourself, "Where am I right now?" When you ask this, you will probably notice that most of the time your mind is anywhere but in the present. Most minds are usually somewhere else. While it takes practice to bring your focus back to where you are, asking yourself that crucial question is the very trigger you will need to help you come back to your breath. If you can keep on remembering to come back to your breath, it will remind you to be present to enjoy what is going on around you. In time it will also help you feel less harried, worried, and stressed.

If you want to know what your soul feels like, being present at various times during the day will be a giant step toward that goal. The more you practice being right here, right now, the more you will love doing it, because it will heighten the pleasure of daily life.

You once knew someone who was given a life-threatening diagnosis. When he told you about it, he was no longer interested in the details of his past or what might happen in the future. In fact, he became extremely motivated to be right here, right now. More than anything, he wanted to savor his life and his family. He wasn't even interested in doing the things he had always wanted to do. Instead, he just wanted to enjoy his life in small ways while he still had time. He spoke of becoming more aware of the mundane things he had always taken for granted – a sunset, the smell of newly cut grass, the touch of his wife's hand. He reminded you that being present in this way is one of the keys to living a full life. And for that moment, he was your teacher, helping you to remember not to take your precious life for granted.

One of the highest states of living one can attain is to become fully aware in the present moment. It doesn't matter if you're shopping at Walmart, working at your job, or watching your dogs at play. When you are in the present, the joy of being alive comes to fruition. By being fully present in your life, you honor the life you have chosen. Inhale the moment you are in right now, Dear One, because there is no greater moment than this one.

Ever since you came here, you have wanted to remember yourself as an eternal soul whose primary purpose is to become aware of itself while in human form. By being more present in life, you have the opportunity to realize that you *are* a Divine Consciousness becoming conscious of itself. Watching life unfold as you create it, you can realize that you *are* the vastness and peacefulness of life. By allowing yourself to be fully present, you will be led to know yourself as the Divine Presence you really are. And as you continue to know yourself as both human and Divine, you will find yourself celebrating the joy of knowing that the fulfillment you have been looking for all your life has been right here in front of you all along, in the present moment.

The "Knowing"

Dear One,

As the ten-year-old girl stood on the dock watching two teenage girls swim across the pond, she thought, "I can do that. It's a long way, but all I have to do is keep my arms and legs moving, and I'll make it." As the thought passed, she felt an unexpected ache in her stomach. The feeling was so heavy that she hesitated. Something inside her said, "Don't do this." As I watched her listen to the feeling I was sending her, she made a free will choice and dove headlong into the water. Halfway across the pond, her little arms began to tire, and she panicked. She knew she was in trouble and cried out for help. But the more she struggled, the faster she sank. She could do nothing to save herself and, gasping for air, it struck her that she was too young to die. Then, when she no longer had the strength to struggle anymore, she felt someone lift her head out of the water. Fighting for air, she grabbed the teenage girl and pushed her under. In what seemed like hours, but was only seconds, she heard her rescuer say, "It's okay. Don't push me down. Just relax. We're going to make it." And they did. You were saved, Dear One, by a soul brave enough to risk her life to save another.

To this day, you still remember the feeling you had before jumping off the dock. Your entire being told you not to. You heard the message loud and clear, yet you ended up only three gasps away from losing this lifetime. I call this feeling "the knowing." All human beings have their own feeling of knowing, but they are often afraid to believe it and act on it, or they simply don't want to do what their knowing tells them. How many times have you heard, "Something in me told me not to do it, but I did it anyway." That "something" they speak of is the intuitive voice of their soul telling them to pay attention. Your soul is your internal GPS system that alerts you when you are going in a direction that will not serve you well. This same voice can also encourage you to take a risk that will be good for you, such as the time you left your teaching position to pursue a singing career. Although in some ways you were afraid to do it, this message was not at all like the gnawing feeling you had on the dock. Instead, you felt the excitement of anticipating an adventure. It seemed intuitively like the right thing to do, even though you knew there were certain risks.

The kind of knowing I speak of, Dear One, is difficult to describe. It is a remembrance that emanates from your soul with no visible proof. It is your intuitive sixth sense, your super-conscious God Mind, the mind of Me. It is the place inside you where you know everything. Your God Mind is always open to you. It flows like a river, and all you have to do is jump in. If you perceive the truth of knowing with only your five senses, you are missing out on a world of knowledge, joy, and fulfillment. It would be like having a beautiful garden of flowers in front of you and being able to see only the marigolds. To witness the vastness of life through the eyes of your soul, Dear One, you must be willing to invest in your intuitive self.

Your knowing will always nudge you to feel the truth of who you are. The more deeply you go within yourself, the more the veil of forgetting lifts, making your knowing even stronger. This is why, throughout this book, I have stressed the importance of being in touch with your feelings. Otherwise, you will not be able to determine which feelings spring from your human self and which emanate from Me. Your *intuitive* feelings always come from Me.

Those who are willing to explore the venture of knowing themselves more deeply as a soul must begin by paying closer attention to feelings that are sent by the soul. Clearly, you are becoming increasingly proficient at distinguishing between your energies and Mine; yet, there are times when you let your "shoulds" take over your knowing. Writing this book is a good example. You think to yourself, "I should work on my book today. I usually feel better when I do, and I need to move forward with it." This seems like a good idea, but at the same time you are feeling a stronger inclination to play, rest, or read a good novel. With your own book still waiting to be written, you tend to find such temptations "unproductive." Then you are faced with the question: how do you know whether the signal to rest or play is coming from your soul or from a resistance to writing the book? To know the answer, you need to ask Me, and most often I respond by sending you that "gut feeling" well known to many. So, Dear One, ask your stomach the question and see what it says. If you get a feeling of dread or negativity, you are heading in the wrong direction. If your gut feels a sense of relief, you are being guided in the right direction. When you asked, "Should I continue working on my book today?" there was no resulting sense of excitement and joy. In fact, you could almost hear yourself saying, "Oh no." When you asked if you should take time off, you began to cry. That was your answer. They were not tears of sadness, but of relief. Your tears were telling you, "I'm tired. I need a break and it's okay for me to give this to myself."

You made the decision to follow your knowing, and when you did, two things happened. First, you came back to your book two weeks later feeling refreshed and excited to continue writing. Second, during those two weeks you discovered new ideas for the book that would have eluded you had you not followed your intuition. You see, Dear One, your soul always knows what's best for you. It never leads you down the wrong path. All you have to do is listen. A simple rule to follow is this: If something doesn't feel right for you, don't do it. If something feels right, then follow your intuition. If you follow it and your feeling changes, then turn around and go back. It's as simple as that.

Your intuitive feelings are only one kind of knowing. There is another knowing that goes beyond a human's awareness and understanding. As such, it is not an intuitive feeling. It is a knowledge you have and you don't know how you know it. This can come in the form of a thought that pops into your head without your understanding why, making you wonder, "Where did *that* come from?"

For example, sometimes the phone will ring and you know who it is before you answer it. Last month, someone you hadn't thought about for years suddenly came into your mind. Four days later you learned that he had died. This kind of knowing happens to people all the time, although many shrug it off as coincidence. Yet, how many times have you thought of someone for no apparent reason and within days, or even hours, he or she contacts you? All knowing, Dear One, is part of the osmosis process of the God Mind blending with your conscious mind and leaving an imprint. In essence, it is Me knowing something ahead of time and channeling this knowledge to you. It is not something your humanness can understand, because it emanates from your spiritual, rather than your physical, dimension.

When you begin to pay more attention to what you write off as "coincidence" and see it as a way your soul communicates with you, you will begin to trust that you are connected to a greater force working for your betterment. Although trusting such knowing requires effort and practice, it can be an exciting and worthwhile venture. Therefore, when an unforeseen thought suddenly comes to mind, consider that I could be trying to tell you something. It takes no effort to at least flirt with this idea. Sometimes I might plant a seed in your mind to help you trust this knowing. Other times I might plant it to protect you, as I did for the ten-year-old who was about to dive into the pond.

The other day you were given an opportunity to trust your knowing. While you were enjoying a bike ride, the word "car" suddenly popped into your head. You looked around, but there was no car in sight. Instead of dismissing this thought as nothing, however, you decided to heed that word by becoming more mindful. Within minutes, a car pulled out of its driveway, and not seeing you, came close to hitting you. You were able to stop in time and move to the side of the road because you were on the lookout, just in case. Your vigilance kept you safe because you were thinking that the unexpected could happen. Soon after that, the word, "dog" flooded your mind. Once again, even though there was no dog in sight, you made the conscious decision to think about what you would do if a dog did come your way. You made a plan in your head and kept your eyes open. When you were almost home, a dog came out of the woods running full speed toward you. Instead of panicking, you implemented your plan, which was to ignore it and keep on riding. Happily, there was no misadventure. At that moment, you laid your hand on your heart and said, "Thank you." I knew you were thanking Me and I certainly appreciated that, not only for the acknowledgment, but also for your willingness to listen and know that I am here and ready to guide you at all times. You see, Dear One, you and I are constantly co-creating every day of your life, and life is so much more fun when you know it, as well.

When you begin to accept and trust the knowing that is much greater than yourself, all kinds of delightful experiences will come your way. Sometimes they are quite ordinary and other times they are incredibly profound. Once in a while, because you are willing to listen, I tell you things you could not possibly know through your human awareness. I do this to give you the opportunity to take your knowing to a deeper level. One of those times happened a few years ago when you were waiting to get your nails done. As you observed the woman ahead of you, the thought popped into your head that she had lived many Egyptian lives. You chuckled at this thought and paid it no mind, thinking how odd it was. But then you became curious. What if the thought came from a part of you that knew something you didn't? What if this was your "knowing" on a different level? Hmm. You realized that the only way you would know for certain would be to confide this thought to the woman. This was not something you had ever done before, nor were you comfortable doing it. However, you were so intrigued that you decided to take the risk and speak to her, no matter how she might respond. As you related what had come into your mind, she looked at you in astonishment and said, "All my life I have had the desire to go to Egypt. I don't know why but I have always felt an attraction to that part of the world. So last month I took a three-week trip to Egypt. It felt like home, as though I had lived there before. How did you ever know this?" You replied, "I didn't. I just had this thought and decided to test it out." Let me say, Dear One, that I sent you this particular message because I know you believe in past lives. Don't expect that another's soul will send such messages if the same belief does not reside in them. The soul can only reach its human counterpart on their given level.

The miracle of this experience, Dear One, was not in your revelation to this woman. It was a lesson of trust for you. By revealing this information, you were able to see firsthand the workings of your soul and its gift of knowing something you could not possibly have known through your human awareness. In this case, it was My way of helping you find the trust you needed in Me at that particular time in your life.

If more people would trust their knowing, they would experience and believe more deeply in who they really are. Every person on this Earth has the same knowing that you do. It is just a matter of how willing one is to practice it. Like anything in life, the more you practice, the better you become. And the better you get at it, the more you trust it.

Dear One, know that when something rings true and feels right, it is because you are remembering your deeper place within. This is Me encouraging you to trust in what you already know, because knowing is part of the remembering process. When you walk on the path of your knowing, you abide in your soul. I will never lead you astray. I am here to be your Guide, your Mentor, and the Captain of your ship. I am your Soul-mate in the purest sense of the word. As you continue to find the courage, trust, and faith in the God within, you will know that all things are possible. You are not here to understand everything in life. It is impossible to do so. But you *are* here, Dear One, to have an open mind and heart, so that you can remember who you are. And with that remembrance comes the faith that will not only move mountains, but will also be the force that guides you through life so you can live and feel the truth of the joyous soul you are.

Becoming the Divine Observer

Dear One,

Many years ago, you were sitting alone in a restaurant, having lunch, when suddenly you heard uproarious laughter coming from a table across the room. As you looked up, you saw five Down's syndrome teenagers from a local daycare center sitting with their supervisors. Your first thought was about their affliction, which made your first *feeling* one of pity. It was then you and I had a mental conversation.

"How awful for these poor children, who probably will never marry, go to school, or become independent. What a difficult existence – never growing up and learning about life," you thought.

I replied, "Is that not a judgment, Dear One? How do you know they are not learning in life? Is it just because they are not learning in the same way you are?"

"Hmm," you said. "That's true. In some way, they *are* learning, but how dreadful it must be to have to be taken care of for the rest of your life."

"Really?" I replied. "Isn't that what your inner child has always wanted? When you think about it, is it really such a bad thing?"

"Well, when you put it like that, I have always wanted to be taken care of, and at times I still do, but not *that* way."

"Of course not. In this lifetime it would *not* be your way because you have chosen a different set of circumstances. Have you ever considered, however, that this might be the right and perfect situation for *their* particular soul growth? If you truly believe that souls choose their lives before they come to Earth, then where does this situation fit in? Do you really believe your truth, or are you making exceptions?"

"I do believe it," you replied, "and now I see that I allowed my humanness to judge the situation instead of seeing it from a higher perspective."

"I want you to do something, Dear One. Look closer."

As you did, you noticed that their laughter filled the restaurant with such joy that other patrons looked up and began to smile. It was contagious. The closer you looked, the more you noticed the sparkle in their eyes and their utter delight when the waitress brought their food. You saw the supervisors tuck napkins under their chins with loving care. You watched as they wiped the mashed potatoes off their happy faces, and saw the hugs they got in return. You were so moved by the pure happiness emanating from that side of the room that you began to tear up. When you looked closer and released the judgment of seeing those beautiful souls as lacking in some way, you saw only love. You were moved because you took the opportunity to observe this situation from a different point of view. You no longer felt that these teenagers' lives should have been different. Instead, you were witnessing souls who had chosen this kind of life for a distinct reason, either for their own evolution, yours, or both. By becoming the Divine Observer of this situation rather than letting your humanness judge it, you were able to see it through the eyes of your soul.

I will tell you, Dear One, that each of those beautiful souls across the room came to this Earth to experience love in a very different way. They had no need to know love as you do, or to be as independent as you are. They came here to let love take care of them. And from My perspective, why isn't that absolutely wonderful? As you continued to watch this table of incredible beings, you realized that those caring for them were also beautiful souls who, for their own evolution, came into this life to be of service. By being willing to listen to the conversation in your head and by observing the situation through your Divine eyes, you were able to move from the human perspective to the spiritual one. By the time you left the restaurant, you felt uplifted and marveled at the miracle of life and how the Creator designed it. You felt blessed at having been given such a gift that day. I also want you to know, Dear One, that you gave that gift to yourself because you took the time to pay attention to what was going on in your head. This, in turn, gave you the opportunity to experience what it feels like to be who you really are. If you can look at situations from this perspective, life can take on new and wonderful meanings.

This particular instance is an example of becoming a Divine Observer as related to an external situation. The other level of becoming a Divine Observer involves investigating yourself from an inner perspective. As always, it will mean releasing judgment. Becoming a Divine Observer is not easy for most human beings because they cannot let go of their need to judge. However, you cannot become the Divine Observer you want to be without doing so. So I will give you a sure way to help you release judgment and continue on this path.

As a child, you used to lie on your grandmother's root cellar doors and watch the clouds. You loved imagining that they had various animal shapes as they floated by. You had no reason to judge one cloud over another or want to make them go away. To become the Divine Observer of *you*, Dear One, you must look at your thoughts and feelings as though you are looking at the clouds. Do not judge one good or another bad, and do not will them to disappear. You need only observe and accept them as you did the clouds. You can use that same awareness you had in the restaurant to observe what is going on inside of you from a higher perspective.

To help you do this, I'm going to outline an exercise that has often served you well throughout your life. You may use this exercise with any feeling you are experiencing, whether joyful or unpleasant. While it is a wonderful exercise to use with the former, for the purpose of this letter I will focus on the latter, since this is where more help is needed in your world.

Here it is: Whenever you are feeling upset, whether it is irritation, sadness, or worry – try to find a quiet place to sit for a few moments. If this is not possible, you can still practice this exercise anywhere. Sit quietly and allow yourself to feel the upset within. Accept it for what it is. Then visualize a golden-white light emanating from inside of you and enveloping the entire outside of your body. Know that this light is Me wrapping My Divine arms around you. As I embrace you, I am also watching you experience your upset. Visualize yourself being observed by Me. This will acknowledge that you are having a human feeling while at the same time surrounding yourself with the wellbeing of your Divinity. I am the peace that is ever present within you and always waiting for you. My essence never changes. I am peace, joy, and love when you are happy, and I am peace, joy, and love when you are not. You can access this peace at any time, no matter what it is you are experiencing.

As you sit, knowing that both the Divine and the human are in your sight, place this golden-white light of peace around the non-peace in you. Whatever the feeling, even the tiniest irritation – acknowledge it and feel the peace. Most important, picture Me in your mind's eye, observing and surrounding you inside and out with this peace. It would be as if I were behind and above you looking over you with love. Know that these are your spiritual eyes observing your human self. In other words, it is the real you looking at you. You will soon discover that you have the ability to overcome, or at least diminish, the upset by just observing it from this higher perspective. This is because all upset is created by the ego, and the ego does not like to be exposed to observation. It knows inherently that there is something greater than it is. When that greater entity, your soul, is being engaged by your free will self, the ego will run away and hide for the time being. The upset will diminish, and what remains is the peace.

When you first began this exercise a few years ago, you were amazed at the results. I tell you this, Dear One, because the soul of you will always triumph over your humanness. When you can step back from your upsets and allow the Divine Observer in you to come out, the annoyances of life will gradually diminish, and your happiness will gradually increase. It is a very courageous thing to take responsibility for your emotional life and diminish its turmoil. If humans would realize that they can use the Divine Observer within to help them choose wellbeing over turbulence, they would progress toward their evolution in leaps and bounds.

You are the great Divine Observer of life, Dear One, the eye witness to everything that goes on around you and within you. When you practice watching yourself from a higher perspective, you will have more access to the Deeper Intelligence within you. When you choose to become the Divine witness to your thoughts and feelings, rather than the reactor, you will be able to maintain a higher perspective, which will help you immensely in any situation throughout your life.

Always remember that I am your Haven. You can come to me when you feel that no one understands you or when you feel fearful, lost, unhappy, or worried. Know that you have the ability to tap into your peace and wellbeing at any time. By remembering that you are a soul first and a human second, you will allow yourself to experience the excitement that comes from being a Divine Observer living in a human world. Then you will stand on the highest rung of the ladder and experience yourself as both Heaven and Earth, human and Divine. You will know that you are a powerful Creator given the opportunity to shape your Destiny and create an outstanding life. This is your birthright, Dear One. Love it, and use it.

Taking the High Road

Dear One,

It is no coincidence that you and I have arrived here together at the High Road. Each letter has been like a signpost leading us here. Everything I have said to you thus far has been in preparation for taking the High Road of integrity. The previous themes of acceptance, non-judgment, responsibility, soul growth, courage, process, and self-love – to name a few – have prepared you to walk the road less-traveled. You will get on and off this path many times in your life, which is all right. The fact that you are willing to follow it in the first place means everything. As I describe the High Road to you, know that I do not expect perfection. Detours are part of being human. The High Road is something to aspire to. While living a life of integrity may mean many different things to many different people, the following is what it means from My higher perspective:

When you take the High Road in life, there is no longer any need to lie, for you do not have to hide from anything or anyone. Because you no longer come from a mindset of deprivation, there is no need to steal, whether it is a physical object or an idea. When you take the High Road, you are not interested in gossip because you remember that you are One with all others. You know inherently that when you put someone down, you are doing so to yourself. Taking the High Road means releasing judgment from your life, beginning with *you*. When you stop judging yourself, you stop judging others, because you understand that not everyone on this planet is supposed to exist at the same grade level.

Because you believe in your ability to cope with anything, taking the High Road means working on diminishing worry. It means that you have to let go of the concept of lack because you realize that there is enough abundance to go around and you remember that you have the potential to create it. Walking down this road entails taking responsibility for what you think and feel without blaming others. It means you are accountable for the choices you make in life. When you take the High Road, you know without a doubt that ego will try to deter you from your path. Sometimes you will succumb to it, and at other times you won't, but you will always find the courage to get back on the road.

When you are willing to take the High Road, Dear One, it means that you are willing to pay attention to your fears and how they can diminish your happiness. You will include loving yourself in your daily ritual, knowing that this will always lead you to Me in some form or other. When you are willing to dedicate yourself to loving you, you will desire to know God in a more personal way.

Taking the High Road is about living a life of integrity, not in words, but through your actions. Living as a soul first and a human second, means aligning your actions with your spiritual truth. It means your actions are based on a higher perspective, allowing you to let go of pettiness, revenge, and the need to manipulate and control. When you walk down the High Road, you place your spiritual nature above your human one.

I know this is not an easy task, but I didn't come into this lifetime to experience "easy" as such. You see, Dear One, I haven't always taken the High Road in other lives. During those lifetimes the free will of my human personality did not choose to know itself as fully as you have. Therefore, I have come into this lifetime with you to find my way to the High Road. I have come to help you remember yourself as a beautiful, eternal soul who has always wanted to make a difference in the world, no matter how small. By living your life from a place of integrity, you are igniting your Light within and helping Me to follow My path.

I know that you will hesitate to write what I say next, but it is important that you do so. You see, Dear One, here is an example of your need to be humble rather than allow Me to express your magnificence and how I feel about you. What I am about to say is something many souls want to tell their Earthly counterparts, if only their human personalities would listen.

I want you to know that this life with you is extraordinary for Me. It is a joy to be remembered, and I am grateful that you are willing to make the effort to live your truth on the High Road of life. I thank you for your cooperation, dedication, and hard work. I thank you most of all for listening. Without that, this book would not exist. I rejoice in the co-creative process of our life together for we have *both* grown. And I want you to know something else. From the moment you took your first precious breath, there has been no one who loves you more than I.

Love is the Measure of the Journey

Dear One,

Love is the essence and lubricant of life. It has the power to heal any situation and overcome any fear. While it has many levels and many expressions, there is no such thing as a small gift of love. All love is magnificent, whether it is love for a child, a kitten, or a tree. It can be found in the smallest places, and it can turn something ordinary into something Divine. Because it is the only feeling that comes directly from God, love reigns supreme over all other feelings. In fact, all other feelings are either an extension of that love or exemplify the lack of it. In essence, our book is about love. It is a love story between a soul and its human personality, also known as the love between you and God. It is the only story you will ever encounter that has no ending. It represents the love that has brought you here and the love that will take you Home.

Love is food for the soul. Every soul yearns for love because love is fundamental to its nature. This desire to express love spills over to the human personality and is absorbed as though by osmosis. Humans simply do not recognize it as such. They think love is a human quality. In truth, love is who they really are, a soul longing to experience its essence in physical form. Love is the most powerful feeling in the Universe. Look at all the songs in your world that have the word "love" in them -- thousands upon thousands, more so than any other word in your language. Since the dawn of Mankind, songs have been sung about the thrill of love or the heartbreak when it is gone. This is no coincidence, Dear One, because love is the only true feeling that exists. On a very deep level, humans remember this. But because you live in the Earthly world of duality, you experience love and all its opposites. You are given the opportunity to either express love or withhold it. In My Heavenly Home, however, there is no such choice. There is only love.

Your world continues to expound on love and the lack of it through television and cinema. Romantic comedies depict love lost and regained, while dramas often focus on the absence of love. Today, violence runs rampant on TV and movie screens dominated by scenes of humans being raped, maimed, blown up, and tortured. Your world is becoming increasingly de-sensitized to the fictitious killing of others, which is now considered main-stream entertainment.

But I tell you this, Dear One. If your movie theaters were to show kittens and puppies being maimed, blown up, or tortured, your Society would have none of it. This would be an outrage. I can tell you unequivocally that no such movie would be tolerated, which is why there is no such movie that exists. Why is that? Ironically, it has to do with love. Humans feel more unconditional love from animals than they do from each other, which is why you would never see the killing of them on screen. Needless to say, your world is in dire need of a makeover when it comes to love. If you want it to become a place where hurting others is no longer tolerated on or off the screen, you will need to fill that world with more love. What I say to you next may sound quite simple, but love really *is* the answer to everything.

As always, love starts with yourself. It is important to take an inventory of your life to see where love fits in. How willing are you to give it, and how willing are you to receive it? Sometimes you may even need to ask the question, "How willing are you to admit that you may even be afraid of it?" Believe it or not, Dear One, there are many in your world who are afraid of the intimacy of love. This is why there is nothing more important at this time in your life and in your world than becoming the most loving human being you possibly can. To help you attempt this, you only have to ask yourself one very important question. In any situation, ask yourself, "What would love do now?" The answer to that question will always put you on the right path to becoming a more loving human being. All you have to do is act on it.

When you want to feel more love in your life, Dear One, bring back a memory of having felt loved once before and surround yourself with that image. Know that love can be present at any time in your life, for it never leaves you. By enveloping yourself in a loving memory, you can also send out a feeling of love to another. Because it works the same for others as it does for you, I guarantee that the love you send out will find its way to the intended destination. And if you want to spread more love throughout your world, wrap the same feeling of love around you and send it out to bring the greatest good to all involved. The Universe will receive it and send it back into the world. This is how people can heal themselves and Humanity. This is the power of Love. It is not that complicated. It just needs to be awakened and used.

If you pay close attention to what is going on around you, you will see how love is constantly present in everyday life and how it can uplift you. See what happens when you use the word "love" more frequently in your self-talk. For example, when something wonderful happens to you or another, say with great joy, "I love it when that happens!" When you see the majesty of a hawk that has come for a visit, say with great appreciation, "I love it when that happens!" When your friend takes you to lunch, when the sun shines on your face, or even when you've made a mistake and learned from it, repeat your mantra with exultation, "I love it when that happens!" And when you start to cry because you're overwhelmed by all the love you're feeling, whisper through your tears, "I love it when this happens." The more you acknowledge the presence of love in your life, even in the smallest instances, the more you will connect to your soul and truly experience who you really are.

Love is your power, Dear One. Don't ever be afraid to receive it and take it completely. Take the time to love your life. Enjoy what life has to offer, whether it is the sight of snow on the mountains or the waves of the ocean. Embrace loving a hot meal on a cold day or a cold meal on a hot one. Feel the pleasure of a beautiful piece of music, and the smell of lilacs. Look beyond a person's exterior and imagine their true identity to be a loving soul. Try as best you can to love everything and everyone that has brought you here up to this point in time, no matter how painful or beautiful. For, even in the midst of darkness, there has always been and will always be a point of Light and love for you to hold onto. If you look for it, it will be there.

When I return Home after leaving this physical existence, I will witness how much love I was able to give and receive in this lifetime. I will behold how much I remembered who I was by how much I was able to love. When I look back at this lifetime, I will measure its success by how much I was able to love. Love is the ultimate measure of the Earthly journey, Dear One, and when you are on the other side of the veil, you will fully remember that love is all there is. This is why all of us have chosen the journey of Earth. We have come to express our true nature. We have come to give it, receive it, and watch its healing power in action.

If everyone would find enough love in their hearts to recognize the beauty of their own souls, they would know that love *does* make the world go round. Love *is* all you need and that love is more than just a "many-splendored thing." It *is* what the world needs now. With all your strength and courage, Dear One, find a way to choose love as often as you can. For in so doing, not only will you remember who you are, you will also recapture the longing you seek, which is to once again feel the Magnificent Love of God.

Section VII:

Open This Letter
When All Else Fails

Everything Is All Right: A Letter of Hope

Dear One,

The most exciting and momentous time period Mankind has ever experienced is in motion right before your eyes. Do not be fooled by the illusion that your world is falling apart and crumbling to its demise. It is not. It is in the midst of significant change, a transformation to a higher escalation of energy that will permit the human race to attain its fullest potential. The old ego-based structures are beginning to disintegrate, and corruption, lies, and secrecy are becoming exposed. This is occurring worldwide in religious, government, and cultural settings. At the same time, spiritual truths are persistently emerging from the rubble. Change is transpiring on all levels right now because it has to in order for Mankind to wake up. Since the state of your world is Man's creation, if this world is to transform itself into something better, Mankind will have to make the necessary adjustments to strive for the truth.

Because chaos always precedes change, many disruptions are taking place in your world at this point in time. There is an internal surrender, a letting go of that which is no longer physically and emotionally needed, which is causing confusion and loss for many. With this new energy, what worked for the psyche a few years ago no longer works today. Beliefs are being questioned, relationships are ending, and new ones are beginning. Thoughts of what one really wants in life are being scrutinized and taken more seriously than ever before. Society is less willing to follow the old rules of "the

Establishment," and is instead creating a new definition of what is truth. Your world, and everyone in it, Dear One, is in a process of transformation, and nothing can stop it.

Consequently, this is a magical time in your world, not a tragic one. Humanity is being "reborn," not in the Christian sense, but in the sense of what it can be, rather than what it was. It is a time when you have the power to change anything in your life, and a time of clarity to realize that power. You, and everyone in your world, has been blessed and released to a new evolutionary spiral. The Universe has moved up a notch and is taking Mankind with it. Everything is being brought into balance.

With all change, however, comes resistance. Therefore, what you see coming into play in your world right now is the fight to continue the same old thought patterns and ways of life that perpetuate negativity, suffering, greed, and war. When taken to the extreme, this kind of thinking leads to prophesies of Doomsday. Then, rather than seeing this new energy of change and transformation as a step toward the enlightenment of Man, it is viewed as the annihilation of Man. Yet at the same time, there are many in your world who do not want to keep things the same, and who are promoting new thoughts and actions of love and Oneness to benefit Mankind.

Your world is literally in the midst of transition from the fear tactic of the Piscean Age to the love tactic of the Aquarian Age. And since your world is only thirty-five years into the 2,600-year-old Age of Aquarius, it is yet at the very beginning of this energetic influence. This is why the great tug of war in your world must continue for quite some time, so that the old can make way for the new.

Although it may seem as if Mankind will never get there, I am here to encourage the thought that it can and it will. If you look closely at Society, you can see the contrast between the immanent changes and the factions that oppose change. The movie industry, for one, manifests the effects of this dichotomy. More than at any other time, "end of the world" disaster films have become immensely popular, while movies depicting hope, afterlife, and Man's ability to love one another are also thriving at the box office. While television still clings to themes of violence, we are beginning to see programs that touch on spirituality, as well. Mediums, psychics, angels, and scripts affirming that one can have a direct communication with God are more prevalent than ever before. Years ago, such material would not have been considered acceptable.

The most dramatic change in your world, however, is coming from literature. Not long ago, to find books on dreams or spirituality you would have had to look in the occult section of your local bookstore, next to witchcraft. Now, thirty years later, booksellers have entire sections dedicated to all levels of understanding the self from a higher perspective. These are only some of the changes that are happening in their right and perfect time.

Dear One, you are witnessing a time when the veil between the ethereal world (that which you call the spiritual dimension of Heaven) and the physical world of Earth is being drawn aside. The line between Spirit and human is thinning. It is a time when the soul of each of you wants to be heard and recognized. More than in any other era in history, it is a time when Mankind is permitted to discard his illusions, whatever they may be. The years to come will give Humanity the opportunity to take responsibility and realize the power it has to create a more loving world. For thousands of years the ego of the human personality has guided the choices that have been made, not only by individuals, but also by virtue of mass consciousness. Today, your world is in the throes of understanding its relationship to the Creator and moving from an understanding of an external God to an understanding that God lives internally within each one of you. You are here to remember that your soul is the true conductor of the orchestra of life, and that this is a time when the soul can teach the human personality how life really works. In this way, new decisions and creations can be made toward finding a higher dimension of reality. Eons from now, Earthly beings will know that they are deliberate Creators in partnership with the Creator. So you see, Dear One, the world *is* changing, and we are at the forefront of a New Age that marks a momentous development in human existence.

I want to reassure you that right now, whether at the tail end or the beginning of someone's life, every individual on this planet is here to experience this new energy. Every soul has planted itself exactly where it's supposed to be for the betterment of its own soul growth and that of the world. Each soul will reach its own evolution in its right and perfect time because its design has already been determined. Without exception, no soul will be lost or left behind in this Grand Design. This is the Divine Grace of the Creator, and it cannot be any different.

One day, your world will experience a major shift from the consciousness of separation, to the consciousness of Oneness – from the dominance of the ego personality, to the realization of the Divine within. Human beings will no longer have to fear suffering and pain, for they will know that suffering is not the way Home. Peace, joy, and love are the way Home, and there will come a time when everyone will remember this. If you will look at the change happening in your world in its most positive light, you will find the perfection in it, as I do. There is nothing more perfect than for Man to see his own Light and realize that he is One with the Divine Force. This will happen in its right and perfect time.

One of the greatest lessons in life is to realize that everything will turn out all right, even though the outcome may not necessarily be what you consciously want or expect. If you can hold on to that kernel of faith, you will see how the magic of God works. Believing something when it appears as though there is nothing to believe in is one of the highest lessons of evolution anyone can learn. Then no longer will there be any need to worry about what is happening "out there." So make what's happening in your life – right here, right now – a joy, for in doing so you will create the "out there."

You've learned everything about the ship, Dear One. Now, it's time for you to sail. You are the master of your own ship and by your own Divine right have the right to steer its direction at any point in time. Live your life as a celebration. Enjoy every moment of your path, for it is the enjoyment of every step along the way that makes the journey rich. Delight in the bounty of it. Continue to look for what is right in your life and in your world. Focus on being as happy as you can as often as you can, for in doing so you will create the space for everything to fall into place and take care of itself. Know without a doubt that your world is falling into the hands of its own salvation. No matter what happens in your life or in your world, the results are already in. Everything is, has always been, and will always be, all right.

From the moment I entered this lifetime our unique journey began, and it has proved to be everything I hoped it would be. I want you to know, Dear One, that no matter which lifetime, I will continue to choose you over and over again. Although your form will differ from what it is now, the remembrance of this extraordinary life with you will always be with Me. Our journey will never end, for I am always in motion, ever expanding, and constantly creating. I am the "forever" part of you, the Eternal Divine Consciousness of God that will never cease to grow and evolve. And when I desire to experience the cycle of return once again, a day will come when a newborn baby will take its first breath. This infant will be born all grown up. Housed inside its little body will be a magnificent Light, a piece of the Creator, the Soul of you, ready to fulfill its next purpose.

When you have even the tiniest glimpse of remembering this, Dear One, you will have answered every prayer you've ever had, fulfilled your every wish, and granted yourself the legacy you've always longed for. Most of all, you will have given yourself the most precious gift one can ever receive, the experience of knowing the Sacred You. And then, Dear One, you will finally discover what you've always wanted to know; you will awaken to experiencing your dream of what it is like to live your life somewhere over the rainbow.